AN ACTOR'S HANDBOOK

"I have felt there was nothing for me to do except to devote my labour and energy almost exclusively to the study of Creative Nature. . . . I have acquired a sum of experience in the course of long years of work and this is what I have sought to share with you." —Stanislavski

in series with

by Constantin Stanislavski

by Jean Benedetti

AN
ACTOR'S HANDBOOK

AN ALPHABETICAL ARRANGEMENT OF
CONCISE STATEMENTS ON
ASPECTS OF ACTING

BY CONSTANTIN STANISLAVSKI

EDITED AND TRANSLATED BY
ELIZABETH REYNOLDS HAPGOOD

Methuen Drama

First published in Great Britain in 1990
by Methuen Drama

21 23 25 27 29 28 26 24 22

Methuen Publishing Limited
11-12 Buckingham Gate, London SW1E 6LB

Methuen Publishing Limited Reg. No. 3543167

First published on the 100th Anniversary
of the birth of Constantin Stanislavski,
January 17th, 1963, by Theatre Arts Books

Papers used by Methuen Publishing Limited
are natural, recyclable products made from wood grown in
sustainable forests. The manufacturing processes conform to
the environmental regulations of the country of origin

Printed and bound in Great Britain by
Cox & Wyman Ltd, Reading, Berkshire

A CIP catalogue record for this book
is available from the British Library

ISBN 0-413-63080-3

FOREWORD BY THE EDITOR

In the course of the last few years a number of books, purporting to explain, interpret, or restate in simplified form what Stanislavski really thought and taught, have appeared in America and England. To commemorate the centennial of his birth on January 17th, 1963, it occurred to his principal publisher that a tribute and service to him would be to make available in Stanislavski's *own words* what he himself said about the various facets of the art to which he devoted his whole life, body and soul.

Here, then, is the alphabet of his teaching in concise form. It is based to some extent on a similar "lexicon" published in Moscow and sent to me by his son, but the choice of quotations here is predicated more on their usefulness to theatre people in the West. Much of the material is taken from books previously published in English, but, thanks to the efforts of the archivists in Moscow who have collated all of Stanislavski's papers, including fragments and variations, exceptionally pithy statements for many topics were found and are here translated for the first time.

This volume in no way replaces the full expression of his ideas in his books, which have spread all over the world, to the West and to the East, to India, South America and Japan. It can serve, in this present form, as a handy reference book for the person who is already familiar with the important tenets of his teaching; and, it is to be hoped, it will whet the desire of others to find out through reading the full texts why Stanislavski was such a towering theatre figure and how they themselves can apply his writings.

Since these quotations are drawn from statements made over a long period of years—he lived to be 75—the reader will be aware of certain minor shifts of viewpoint. Because Stanislavski never stood still ("Art and artists must move forward or they will move backward"), he was revising his ideas to his last breath. But the fundamental aim never varied: "to create the life of a human spirit, but also to express it in a beautiful, artistic form." No matter what the angle of approach, his efforts remained constant to achieve "a truth transformed into a poetical equivalent by means of creative imagination."

Stanislavski was fortunate in many ways. He was the son of a wealthy man who could give him the advantages of a broad education, the opportunity to see the greatest exponents of theatre art at home and abroad, the possibility of making his own early experiments in the theatre. He might have remained a brilliant dilettante had he not set his sights on a high goal and never faltered along the hard road leading to it. His personal integrity and inexhaustible capacity for work contributed to make him a professional artist of the first rank. For Stanislavski was also richly endowed by nature with a handsome exterior, fine voice, genuine talent, so that as an actor, director and teacher he was destined to influence and inspire by his own example the many who worked with him and under him, or who had the privilege of seeing him on the stage with the incomparable company of the Moscow Art Theatre of his time.

"Do you realize . . . what is required of an actor, why a real artist must lead a full, interesting, beautiful, varied, exciting and inspiring life?" Those were his words. That was his life.

—E. R. H.

A

ACCENTUATION

Accent is a pointing finger. . . . [It] singles out the key word . . . the high point of the subtext. You know how the third dimension is used to produce depth in a picture. . . . We have as many planes of speech which create perspective in a phrase. The most important word stands out most vividly defined in the very foreground of the sound plane. Less important words create a series of deeper planes. . . . The essential point is not so much the volume as the quality of the accent. Accent can be combined with intonation . . . the latter will colour a word with varied shades of feeling: caressing, malicious, ironical, a touch of scorn, respect and so on. Coordination is [to establish an] harmonious integration . . . of degrees of accentuation volume, for the purpose of setting forth certain words. . . . Another method of emphasis for a key phrase is to change the tempo and rhythm.

—Building a Character

See INTONATIONS AND PUNCTUATION, PAUSES IN SPEECH, SPEECH, SUBTEXT, VOICE VOLUME.

ACTION

On the stage you must always be enacting something; action, motion is the basis of the art . . . of the actor; . . . even external immobility . . . does not imply passiveness. You may sit without motion and at the same time be in full action. . . . Frequently physical immobility is the direct result of inner intensity. So I will . . . put it like this: on the stage it is necessary to act, either outwardly or inwardly. Everything that happens on the stage has a definite purpose. . . . All action in the theatre must have an inner justification, be logical, coherent and real . . . and as a final result we have a truly productive activity. . . .

1. *Physical Actions*

An example: With what is Lady Macbeth occupied at the culminating point of her tragedy? The simple physical act of washing a spot of blood off her hand. . . . In real life also many of the great moments of emotion are signalized by some ordinary, small, natural movement. . . . A small physical act acquires an enormous inner meaning: the great inner struggle seeks an outlet in such an external act. The significance of physical acts in highly tragic or dramatic moments is . . . that the simpler they are, the easier it is to grasp them, the easier to allow them to lead you to your true objective. . . . By approaching emotion in this way, you avoid all forcing and your result is natural, intuitive, and complete.

There are no physical actions divorced from some desire, some effort in some direction, some objective, without one's feeling inwardly a justification for them; there is no imagined situation which does not contain some degree of action of thought; there should be no physical actions created without faith in their reality, consequently a sense of truthfulness. All this bears witness to the close bond between physical action and all so-called "elements" of the inner creative state.

2. Actions Create the Physical Life of a Role

The creation of the physical life is half the work on a role because, like us, a role has two natures, physical and spiritual. To permeate external physical actions with inner essentials, the spiritual life of a part, you must have appropriate material. This you find in the play and in your role . . . because a role, more than action in real life, must bring together the two lives— of external and internal action—in mutual effort to achieve a given purpose.

The spirit cannot but respond to the actions of the body, provided of course that these are genuine, have a purpose, and are productive. . . . Thanks to this approach . . . a part acquires inner content. . . . External action acquires inner meaning and warmth from inner feeling, and the latter finds its expression in physical terms.

To sum up: the point of physical actions lies not in themselves as such but in what they evoke: conditions, proposed circumstances, feelings. The fact that the hero of a play kills himself is not so important as the inner reason for his suicide. If that does not appear or is lacking in interest, his death as such will pass without leaving any impression. There is an unbreakable bond between the action on the stage and the thing which precipitated it. In other words there is a complete union between the physical and the spiritual being of a role. That is what we make use of in our psycho-technique.

3. Pattern of Physical Actions

Write down the list of the physical actions you would undertake if you found yourself in the situation of your imaginary character. Do this same work with the textual role. . . . Write down the list of actions which your character undertakes in accordance with the plot of the play. . . . If the work of the playwright is . . . drawn . . . from the living sources of human nature and human experience and feelings, . . . there will be coincidence at many points between the two lists, especially in all the basic . . . places. . . . To feel yourself even partly in your role and your role even partly in you . . . is the initial step of merging with and living your part.

People who do not understand the line of the physical being in a role laugh when you explain to them that a series of simple, physical, realistic actions has the capacity to engender . . . the life of a human spirit in a role. . . . The point does not lie in these small, realistic actions but in the whole creative sequence which is put into effect, thanks to the impulse given by these physical actions.

—*An Actor Prepares*
—*Creating a Role*
—*Stanislavski's Legacy*

See ELEMENTS OF THE INNER CREATIVE STATE, IMMOBILITY, JUSTIFICATION, PSYCHO-TECHNIQUE, TEMPO-RHYTHM IN MOVEMENT.

ACTOR AS MASTER OF HIS ART

It takes a great artist to convey great feelings and passions—an actor of great power and technique. . . . Without [this last] an actor is incapable of transmitting the universal hopes and tribulations of man.

Lack of understanding and education stamps our art as amateur.

Without a complete and profound mastery of his art an actor cannot carry over to the spectator either the idea, theme or living content of any play.

An actor grows as long as he works. . . . Over a period of years of study [an actor] learns to follow a right course on his own . . . and having learned to do his work properly he becomes a master of his art.

—*Creating a Role*
—*Collected Articles, Speeches, Talks and Letters*
—*Collected Works, Vols. I and VI*

See PSYCHO-TECHNIQUE.

ACTOR AS TRUE ARTIST

A real artist must lead a full, interesting, varied and exciting life. He should know not only what is going on in the big cities, but in the provincial towns, faraway villages, factories and the big cultural centres of the world as well. He should study the life and psychology of the people who surround him, of various other parts of the population, both at home and abroad.

We need a broad point of view to act the plays of our times and of many peoples. . . . To reach the pinnacle of fame an actor has to have more than his artistic talents, he must be an ideal human being . . . capable of reaching the high points of his epoch, of grasping the value of culture in the life of his people, . . . of reflecting the spiritual cravings of his contemporaries.

—*An Actor Prepares*
—*Collected Works, Vol. II*

See IDEAL ARTIST.

ACTOR IN HIS ROLE

Closeness to your part we call perception of yourself in the part and of the part in you. . . . Suppose you go through the whole play . . . find the right actions and accustom yourself to executing them from start to finish. You will then have established . . . the physical life of a part. . . . You must remember . . . that the actions . . . are based on inner feelings. . . . Inside of you, parallel to the line of physical actions, you have an unbroken line of emotions verging on the subconscious. . . . Moreover you can speak for your character in your own person. . . . Bring yourself to the point of taking hold of a new role concretely, as if it were your own life. When you sense that real kinship to your part, . . . your newly created being will become soul of your soul, flesh of your flesh.

—An Actor Prepares
—Collected Works, Vol. VI

See ROLE INSIDE THE ACTOR, ACTION, UNBROKEN LINE.

ACTOR IN OPERA

The objective of the director of an opera is to sift out the *action inherent in the musical picture* and restate this composition of sounds in terms of the dramatic, that is to say the *visual*.

In other words: the action should be determined to a far greater degree by the musical score than merely by the text. The objective of the director is to explain exactly what it is that the composer wished to say when he wrote each phrase of his score, and what dramatic action he had in mind, even though this last may have been only subconsciously in his mind.

I believe there is no basis for dividing operas into operas for singing and musical dramas, for *every* opera is a musical drama. . . . The chief exponent of the action in an opera is the *singer-actor*, not the conductor who often misses the point of dramatic action. . . . The most necessary item of equipment for an operatic artist is, beyond all doubt, a well-placed voice which enables him to sing both *vowels* and *consonants*. The consonants are the more important because they are what carry through the volume of the orchestral accompaniment. The famous singer Battistini owed the volume of his voice to his ability to reinforce his tone through consonants. . . . Tamagno was a dramatic and magnificent Othello in opera because he studied his role with the great tragic actor Salvini, and his musical mentor was Verdi himself. Another master of diction was Chaliapin . . . because he had an intuitive genius he was able to find the right expression and achieved by this means an unparalleled effect.

The production notes of Richard Wagner contain, among other things, the secret of producing an opera. You can bring Wagnerian heroes to life, and make human beings out of them if you can wean them from everything "operatic," and plan their actions in consonance with the *inner meaning* of the music and not the *external* effects.

In opera I take my point of departure from the music, I try to discover what it was that prompted the composer to write his work. Then I try to reproduce this in the action of the singers. If the orchestra plays a prelude, introducing a scene before the action begins we are not content to have the orchestra simply play this, we put it into scenic terms, in the sense of actions, words, phrases. Thus we often use action to illustrate the other instruments which lend colour to the orchestra. If an instrument gives the theme of death, the singer will feel the corresponding emotions. He must not disregard these preludes and use the time to clear his throat or prepare his entrance, he must already be part of the unbroken pattern, of the unfolding life of a human spirit in his part in the play.

The bond with the music must be so close that the action is played in the same rhythm as the music. But this should not be rhythm for the sake of rhythm. . . . I would like this union of rhythm [of action] and music to be imperceptible to the public. We try to have the words merge with the music and be pronounced musically. . . . Since I look upon opera as the collective creation of several arts, the words, the text, diction must be as well worked out as possible on the part of the singer; the public must understand everything that is transpiring on the stage. I even wish to have every word of the ensemble and chorus singing made intelligible.

Chaliapin . . . is the great criterion in opera. Chaliapins cannot be made . . . but the method of Chaliapin should be taught because artists of his calibre come once in a century.

The age of the actor has arrived. He is the top person in the theatre. . . . In opera the need is not only for a good singer, but also a good actor. There must be a matching of the dramatic art with the vocal-musical art.

—*Collected Works, Vol. VI*
—*Stanislavski's Legacy*

See SPEECH, SPEECH TEMPO-RHYTHM, TEMPO-RHYTHM.

ACTOR IN THE FILMS

An actor in the talking films is obliged to be incomparably more skilful and technically expert than an actor on the stage, if the requirements of true art rather than routine accomplishment are to be applied to him. . . . Film actors need real theatre training. They should be bred on a repertory of the world geniuses like Shakespeare, Griboyedov, Gogol, Chekhov and not on ordinary movie scripts.

Film actors are often called upon to play the last sequences in a picture and then the first; they have to die and be born later on. And all this is usually improvised, they rehearse death and then birth.

—Collected Works, Vol. VI

ACTOR IN THE THEATRE

In our theatre, which had its genesis in the Shchepkin traditions, the first place has always been assigned to the actor. For him we did everything that lay in our power.

The theatre exists above all, for the actor, and without him it cannot exist at all.

The only king and ruler of the stage is the talented actor. . . . The main difference between the art of the actor and all other arts is that every other [non-performing] artist may create whenever he is in the mood of inspiration. But the artist of the stage must be the master of his own inspiration and must know how to call it forth at the hour announced on the posters of the theatre. This is the chief secret of our art.

—My Life in Art

See ART OF THE ACTOR AND THE ART OF THE DIRECTOR, INSPIRATION, PSYCHO-TECHNIQUE.

ACTORS USE THEIR OWN FEELINGS

Must we use our own, same, old feelings . . . in every kind of role from Hamlet to Sugar in *The Blue Bird?* What else can you do? . . . Do you expect an actor to invent all sorts of new sensations, or even a new soul, for every part he plays? How many souls would he be obliged to house? . . . Can he tear out his own soul and replace it by one he has rented as being more suitable to a certain part? Where can he get one? You can borrow *things* of all sorts, but you cannot take feelings away from another person. My feelings are inalienably mine, and yours belong to you in the same way. You can understand a part, sympathize with the person portrayed, and put yourself in his place, so that you will act as he would. That will arouse feelings in the actor that are analogous to those required for the part. Those feelings will belong, not to the person created by the author of the play, but to the actor himself. When a real artist is speaking the *Hamlet* soliloquy "To be or not to be" he puts into the lines much of his own conception of life. . . . For him it is necessary that the spectators feel his inner relationship to what he is saying.

The musical scale has only seven notes, the sun's spectrum only seven primary colours, yet the combinations of those notes in music and those colours in painting are not to be numbered. The same must be said of our fundamental emotions.

—*An Actor Prepares*
—*Stanislavski's Legacy*

See JUSTIFICATION, LIVING A PART, TRUE ACTING.

ACTUALITY ON THE STAGE

See SENSE OF TRUTH ON THE STAGE.

ADAPTATION

Adaptation [means] both the inner and outer human means that people use in adjusting themselves to one another in a variety of relationships and also as an aid in affecting an object [person]. Adaptations are made consciously and unconsciously. . . . The most powerful, vivid and convincing [ones] are the products of . . . nature, . . . are almost wholly of subconscious origin.

Each actor has his own special attributes. . . . They spring from varied sources. . . . Each change of circumstance, setting, place of action, time—brings a corresponding adjustment.

All types of communication . . . require adjustments peculiar to each. If people in ordinary . . . life need and make use of a large variety of adaptations, actors need a correspondingly greater number because we must be constantly in contact with one another, and therefore incessantly adjusting ourselves. The quality of the adjustment plays a great part: vividness, colourfulness, boldness, delicacy, shadings, exquisiteness, taste.

In the process of using adaptations there are two moments: first, the selection of an adjustment and, second, its execution, which is largely subconscious. Such adaptations I call semi-conscious.

Our subconscious has its own logic. Since we find subconscious adaptations so necessary in our art, . . . we find that the greatest artists use them. However, even these exceptional people cannot produce them at any given time. They come only in moments of inspiration.

—*An Actor Prepares*

See COMMUNION, INSPIRATION, NATURE.

ADJUSTMENTS

See ADAPTATION.

AFFECTIVE MEMORY

See EMOTION MEMORY, REPEATED FEELINGS.

AMATEUR ATTITUDE

The worst enemy of progress is prejudice: it holds back progress, blocks the way to it. In our art one such example of prejudice is the opinion which defends an amateurish attitude of an actor towards his work. There can be no art without virtuosity, without practice, without technique and the greater the talent, the more they are needed. Amateurs reject technique, not because of conscious convictions but out of unbridled laziness. . . . Indeed, among professional actors there are many who have never changed their amateurish attitude towards acting.

—*Collected Works, Vol. I*
—*My Life in Art*
—*Stanislavski's Legacy*

ANALYSIS

What does . . . analysis consist of? Its purpose is to search out creative stimuli to attract [excite] the actor, lacking which there can be no identification with a part. The purpose of analysis is the emotional deepening of the soul of a part. . . . Analysis studies the external circumstances and events in the life of a human spirit in the part; it searches in the actor's own soul for emotions common to the role and himself, for sensations, experiences, for any elements promoting ties between him and his part; and it seeks out any spiritual or other material germane to creativeness.

Analysis dissects, discovers, examines, studies ways, recognizes, rejects, confirms; it uncovers the basic direction and thought of a play and part, the super-objective, and the through line of action. This is the material it feeds to imagination, feelings, thoughts and will.

Analysis is not solely an intellectual process. Many other elements enter into it, all the capacities and qualities of an actor's nature. . . . Analysis is a means of coming to know, that is, to feel a play. . . . So that in the process of analysis one must use the mind with utmost caution.

Take a firmer hold of physical actions, they are the key to freedom for . . . creative nature and they will protect your feelings from all force. . . . As you are *drawn to* physical actions, you are *drawn away from* the life of your subconscious. In that way you render it free to act and induce it to work creatively. This action of nature and its subconscious is so subtle and profound that the person who is doing the creating is unaware of it. . . . My method draws into action by normal and natural means the subtlest creative forces of nature. . . . This naturally-induced self-analysis is what I wish to stress. . . . Absorbed by immediate physical actions, we do not think about, nor are we aware of, the complex inner process of analysis, which naturally and imperceptibly goes on inside of us.

We have many ways of learning through the analysis of a play and its role. We can retell the content of the play, make lists of facts and events, given circumstances proposed by the author. We can divide a play up into pieces—dissect it, and divide it into layers, think up questions and provide the answers, . . . organize general discussions, arguments and debates, . . . weigh and estimate all facts, find names for units and objectives. . . . All these differing practical methods are part of the single process of analysis, or coming to know the play and your parts. . . . Search for creative stimuli that will provide ever new impulses of excitement, ever new bits of live material for the spirit of a role.

> —*Collected Articles, Speeches, Talks, Letters*
> —*Collected Works Vol. IV*
> —*Creating a Role*

See ACTION, STIMULI TO EMOTION MEMORY.

APHORISM OF PUSHKIN

The great Russian poet Pushkin wrote about dramatists as follows: "Sincerity of emotions, feelings that seem true in given circumstances—that is what we ask of a dramatist."

I add . . . that that is exactly what we ask of an actor. . . . The work of an actor is not to create feelings but only to *produce the given circumstances in which true feelings will spontaneously be engendered.* . . . "Feelings that seem true" . . . refer not to actual feelings but something nearly akin to them, to emotions reproduced indirectly, under the prompting of true inner feelings.

—An Actor Prepares
—Building a Character

See GIVEN CIRCUMSTANCES, SINCERITY OF EMOTIONS.

APPRAISING THE FACTS OF A PLAY

The inner life . . . of the characters is concealed in the outer circumstances of their life, therefore in the facts of the play. The significance of the appraisal of facts lies in its forcing actors to come in contact mentally with each other, making them take action, struggle, overcome or give in to fate or other people. It uncovers their aims, their personal lives, the mutual attitudes of the actor himself, as a living organism in a role, with other characters in the play. . . . It clarifies . . . the inner life of the play.

To appraise the facts is to find the key to the riddle of the inner life of a character which lies hidden under the text of the play.

—Creating a Role

See ACTION, GIVEN CIRCUMSTANCES, PLOT, SUB-TEXT, TEXT.

ARTISTIC ENTHUSIASM

See INNER ARDOUR.

ART OF THE ACTOR AND ART
OF THE DIRECTOR

The actor's creative process starts when he becomes immersed in the play. He should first of all, independently or with the aid of the director, discover the fundamental motive of the play to be produced, . . . the kernel. . . . This basic line of action through all the episodes . . . we call the *through line of action*. . . .

The interpretation of a drama, and the character of its presentation in physical form on the stage is always, and inevitably, to some degree subjective, coloured by both the personal and national traits of the director and of the actors. . . . Having arrived at the kernel, which determines the through line of action of the play, all participants in the future production will be drawn together by it in their creative work: each one to the extent of his capacities, will try to realize in terms of acting that same artistic goal which the playwright set himself in his medium.

As for the outer form of a production—the stage sets, the props, etc.—all that is of value only to the extent that it promotes the expressiveness of dramatic action, the art of the actor; and it should under no circumstances whatsoever draw the public because of any independent artistic quality, something which great artists among our scene designers have wished to do right up to the present time. Stage sets, as well as incidental music, are only auxilliary, supporting factors in theatre art, and it is the duty of the director to draw from them only what is necessary to illuminate the drama being unfolded before the public, and to see that they remain subservient to what the actors are called upon to do.

—*Stanislavski's Legacy*

See CREATIVE INTENT, KERNEL OF A PLAY OR PART, THROUGH LINE OF ACTION.

ARTISTIC TRUTH—NATURAL BEAUTY

Truth on the stage is not the small external truth, which leads to naturalism. . . . It is what you can sincerely *believe* in. . . . Even an untruth must become a truth in the eyes of the actor and the spectator in order to be artistic. . . . *The secret of art is that it converts a fiction into a beautiful artistic truth.* . . . From the moment when the actor and the spectator come to doubt the reality [of the actor's life in the play] truth vanishes, and with it emotion and art. They are replaced by pretense, theatrical falseness, imitation, routine acting. Nature and truth are . . . indivisible.

Natural beauty is the true friend of our being.

Beauty cannot be fabricated, it *is*. . . . It exists in nature all around and in each one of us.

There is no greater beauty in the world than nature itself. One must know how to look at and see beauty. One must learn how to carry beauty over from life and nature on to the stage . . . without crushing or mangling it.

—*Collected Works, Vol. VI*

See NATURE, SENSE OF TRUTH ON THE STAGE, THEATRE.

ATTENTION

1. *Concentration*

Creativeness is first of all the complete concentration of the entire nature of the actor. At one of the performances given by a visiting star . . . I felt the presence of the creative mood in his playing, the freedom of his muscles in conjunction with a great general concentration. . . . His attention was on the stage and the stage alone.

An actor must have a point of attention, and this . . . must not be in the auditorium. The more attractive the object the more it will concentrate the attention. In real life there are always . . . objects that fix our attention, but conditions in the theatre are different, and interfere with an actor's living normally, so that *an effort* to fix attention becomes necessary, . . . to learn anew to look at things, on the stage, *and to see them*.

Intensive observation of an object naturally arouses a desire to do something with it. To do something with it in turn intensifies your observation of it. This mutual inter-reaction establishes a stronger contact with the object of your attention. . . . In watching the acting of great artists . . . their creative inspiration is always bound up with their concentration of attention. . . . When an actor's attention is not turned towards the spectators, . . . he acquires a special hold on them, . . . forcing them to participate actively in his artistic life. . . . The actor who has the trained habit can limit his attention within a *circle of attention,* he can concentrate on whatever enters that circle, and with only half an ear can listen to what transpires outside of it. . . . He can even narrow the circle to produce a state we may call *public solitude.* . . . This circle of attention is usually flexible, it can be enlarged or shrunk by the actor in accordance with whatever must be included for the purposes of the stage action. Inside the limits of the circle there is an immediate and *central object of attention.* . . . *Creativeness on the stage,* whether during the preparation of a part or during its repeated performance, demands complete concentration of all [the actor's] physical and inner nature, the participation of all his physical and inner faculties.

2. Concentrated Sensory Attention

To grasp your object firmly when you are acting you need another type of attention, which causes an emotional reaction. You must have something which will interest you in the object of your attention, and serve to set in motion your whole creative apparatus. It is, of course, not necessary to endow every object with an imaginary life, but you should be sensitive to its influence on you. . . . Imagined circumstances can transform the object itself and heighten the reaction of your emotions to it. . . . You must learn to transfigure an object from something which is coldly reasoned or intellectual in quality into something which is warmly *felt.* We actors have come to call this *sensory attention.* . . . It is particularly valuable in the creative work of preparing "the life of a human spirit in a role."

3. Imaginary Objects of Attention

Inner attention centres on things we see, hear and touch and feel in imaginary circumstances. . . . We see such images with an inner vision. . . . The same is true of our sense of hearing, smell, touch and taste. . . . This abstract life contributes an unending source of material for our inner concentration of attention . . . but imaginary objects demand an even far more disciplined power of attention. . . . Use the exercises, . . . developed for the imagination, as they are equally effective for concentrating attention.

4. *Physical Attention*

Your physical attention [has been drawn] to the movement of energy along a network of muscles. This same kind of attention should be fixed on ferreting out points of pressure in the process of relaxing our muscles. What is muscular pressure or spasm except moving energy that is blocked? . . . It is important that your attention move in constant company with the current of energy, because this helps create an . . . unbroken line which is so essential in our art.

5. *Concentrated Attention and Creative Material*

At the bottom of every process of obtaining creative material is emotion. Feeling, however, does not replace an immense amount of work on the part of our intellects. . . . After you have learned how to observe life around you and draw on it for your work you will turn to . . . the living emotional material on which your main creativeness is based. . . . Impressions . . . from direct, personal intercourse with other human beings, . . . many invisible, spiritual experiences are reflected in our facial expression, in our eyes, voice, speech, gestures, but even so it is no easy thing to sense another's inmost being, because people do not often open the doors of their souls. . . . When the inner world of someone . . . becomes clear to you through his acts, thoughts, impulses, follow his actions closely and study the conditions in which he finds himself.

Here we are dealing with the most delicate type of the concentration of attention and with powers of observation which are subconscious in their origin.

As you progress you will learn more and more ways in which to stimulate your subconscious selves, and to draw them into your creative process, but it must be admitted that we cannot reduce this study of the inner life of other human beings to a scientific technique. . . . Do not look with a cold analytical eye or carry a pencil in your hand. . . . Do not be a cold observer of another's life, but let [your study] raise your own creative temperature.

After prolonged, penetrating observation and study an actor acquires excellent creative material.

—An Actor Prepares
—Building a Character
—Collected Works, Vol. II
—My Life in Art
—Stanislavski's Legacy

See COMMUNION, CONTACT WITH THE AUDIENCE, MATERIAL FOR CREATIVENESS, OBSERVATION, RELAXATION OF MUSCLES, PUBLIC SOLITUDE, UNBROKEN LINE.

AUDIENCE

The more the actor wishes to amuse his audience, the more the audience will sit back in comfort waiting to be amused; . . . but as soon as the actor stops being concerned with his audience, the latter begins to watch the actor. It is especially so when the actor is occupied in something serious and interesting.

Only true acting can completely absorb an audience, making it not only understand but participate emotionally in all that is transpiring on the stage, thus being enriched by an inner experience which will not be erased by time.

To act without an audience is the same as singing in a room without any resonance. . . . To act before a full and responsive audience is like singing in a hall with excellent acoustics. . . . The audience provides

. . . our spiritual acoustics, . . . like a sounding board returning to us living, human emotions. . . . The point is not in the power of an effect but in its quality. . . . It is not the purpose of an actor to make a fleeting impression on the audience. It is much more valuable to have a quiet audience . . . which will receive a lasting imprint.

New methods of creativeness have produced new playwrights and a new kind of audience, which knows not only how to look and be entertained in the theatre, but also how to listen, feel and reflect on what it sees.

These new spectators do not expect writing or acting which is merely externally effective in external plot and action; they look for deep feelings and great thoughts.

Thus the audience is a creative participant in the performance of a play.

—*An Actor Prepares*
—*Collected Works, Vol. V*
—*My Life in Art*

See COMMUNION, CONTACT WITH AUDIENCE.

B

BALLET

Ballet is a beautiful art, but it is not for us dramatic artists. We need something else. We need other plasticity, other grace, another rhythm, another set of gestures, another manner of walking, another method of movement. We must borrow only the amazing capacity for work and the knowledge of how to train the body from the artists of the ballet.

—*My Life in Art*

See BODY TRAINING, PLASTICITY OF MOTION, TUMBLING.

BEATS

[Supposedly a mispronunciation of "bits"—here called units—on the part of early Russian teachers of the Stanislavski system in America.—Editor]

See UNITS.

BODY TRAINING

People generally do not know how to make use of the physical apparatus with which nature has endowed us. They neither know how to develop this apparatus nor keep it in order. Flabby muscles, poor posture, sagging chests, these things we see around us continually. They show insufficient training and an inept use of the physical instrument.

Maybe a body, with bulges in the wrong places, legs so spindly that their owner has to totter, shoulders hunched almost into a deformity, does not matter in ordinary life. In fact we become so accustomed to these and other defects that we accept them as normal phenomena. But when we step on the stage many lesser physical shortcomings attract immediate attention. There the actor is scrutinized by thousands of onlookers as through a magnifying lens. Unless it is his intention to show a character with a physical defect, in which case he should be able to display it in just the proper degree, he should move in an easy manner which adds to rather than detracts from the impression he creates. To do this he must have a healthy body in good working order, capable of extraordinary control. . . . Exercises contribute towards making your physical apparatus more mobile, flexible, expressive and even more sensitive.

Do you admire the physique of the circus strong man? For my part I know nothing more repellent than a man with shoulders that more rightly belong on a bull, with muscles that form great Gordian knots all over him.

Now you are at the crossroads. What direction will you take? Proceed along the line of muscular development of a weightlifter, or follow the requirements of our art? Naturally I must direct you along this latter line.

We now add sculptural requirements to your gymnastic training. Just as the artist with the chisel seeks the right line, the beautiful proportions in the balance of the parts of the statues he creates out of stone, the teacher of gymnastics must try to achieve the same results with living bodies. There is no such thing as an ideal human structure. It has to be made, to that end one must first study the body and understand the proportions of the various parts. When the defects have been found, they must be corrected. . . . By increasing the muscular structure . . . a proper overall form can be established.

Physical culture adepts . . . are not natural, their bodies are not flexible on the stage, nor do they submit to the demands of an inner life. What they convey is in coarse, inartistic form. Boxing can be harsh. Sportsmen are agile only in certain movements required by the special type of sport in which they are engaged. . . . Ideal physical exercises are those which remedy the insufficiencies of nature. . . . Above all it is desirable that no movements undertaken in the course of exercises be lacking in intent.

Expressive body training . . . includes gymnastics, dance, acrobatics [tumbling], fencing (foils, rapiers, daggers), wrestling, boxing, carriage, all the aspects of physical training.

Your powers of expression as an artist will be tested to the limit by the adjustments you must make in relation to the other actors on the stage. For this reason you must give appropriate preparation to your body, face, and voice. . . . I hope this will make you aware of the necessity of your exercises in physical culture, dancing, fencing, and voice placing.

                    —An Actor Prepares
                    —Building a Character
                    —Collected Works, Vol. III

See BALLET, COMMUNION, EXTERNAL TECHNIQUE, FACE, TUMBLING.

C

CARPING CRITICISM

A nagging critic can drive an actor mad and reduce him to a state of helplessness. Search for falseness only so far as it helps you find the truth. Don't forget that the carping critic can create more falsehood on the stage than anyone else, because the actor whom he is criticising involuntarily ceases to pursue his right course and exaggerates truth itself to the point of its becoming false.

A calm, wise and understanding critic is the artist's best friend. He will not nag you over trifles, but will have his eye on the substance of your work.

—An Actor Prepares

See CRITICS, SELF-CRITICISM.

CHARACTERISATION AND TRANSFORMATION

I claim that all actors must be character actors, of course not in the sense of outer, but of inner characteristics. . . . This does not mean [the actor] must lose his own individuality and his personality; it means that in each role he must find his individuality and his personality, but nevertheless be different in every role.

As for inner characterisation, it can be shaped only from an actor's own inner elements. These must be felt and chosen to fit the image of the character to be portrayed. . . . If this is effectively prepared, the outer characterisation should naturally follow. . . . Let every actor achieve this outer characterisation by using material from his own life, from that of others, real or imaginary, by using his intuition, self-observation . . . by studying paintings or books . . . or by noting accidental occurrences—in short from every possible source. . . . But in all this external search an actor must never lose his own identity.

Any role that does not include a real characterisation will be poor, not lifelike, and the actor who cannot convey the character of the roles he plays is a poor and monotonous actor. As a matter of fact, there is no person on earth who does not possess his own individual character. . . . That is why I propose for actors a complete inner and external metamorphosis.

There are actors and especially actresses who do not feel the need of preparing characterisations or transforming themselves into other characters because they adapt all roles to their own personal appeal.

There is a great difference between searching for and choosing in oneself emotions related to a part, and altering the part to suit one's more facile resources.

[An actor] will not give himself up wholly to his part unless it carries him away. When it does so he becomes completely identified with it and is transformed.

Characterisation, when accompanied by a real transposition, a sort of re-incarnation, is a great thing. Since an actor is called upon to create an image while he is on the stage . . . [characterisation] becomes a necessity for all [actors]. In other words all actors who are artists should make use of characterisation.

A capacity to transform himself, body and soul, is the prime requirement for an actor.

—*Building a Character*
—*Collected Articles, Speeches, Talks, Letters*
—*Collected Works, Vols. III and IV*
—*My Life in Art*

See ACTORS USE THEIR OWN FEELINGS, EXTERNAL TECHNIQUE, TYPES.

CHARM

There are certain actors who have only to step on the stage and the public is already enthralled by them. . . . What is the basis of the fascination they exercise? It is an indefinable, intangible quality. . . . It transforms even an actor's deficiencies into assets.

Still . . . when they meet this same actor off the stage even his warmest admirers are disillusioned. . . . It is no wonder the quality is called stage and not natural charm. . . . It is a great advantage to possess it. Yet it is of utmost importance that he [the actor] use this precious gift with prudence, wisdom and modesty. . . . Self-admiration and exhibitionism impair and destroy the power to charm. . . . There are also actors who possess another variety of stage charm. . . . They have only to put on wigs, make-up which entirely masks their own personality and they exercise great stage magnetism. . . . The unlucky actor who lacks theatre attractiveness . . . influences the public against him. . . . Yet such actors are often far more intelligent, gifted, conscientious about their art. . . . Is there no method to develop a certain degree of stage charm? . . . Only to a limited extent. It is accom-

plished by toning down unattractive shortcomings.
. . . It requires close observation, . . . patience and
systematic work. . . . One of the most important helps
is habit. A spectator can become accustomed to the
shortcomings of an actor and they may even take on
the aspect of a certain attractiveness. . . . We often
hear people say: How such-and-such an actor has mel-
lowed!

To a certain extent one may even create stage charm
through the use of an excellent, well-bred manner in
acting as that in itself is attractive.

Art lends beauty and nobility, and whatever is
beautiful and noble has the power to attract.

As I grow older and think about our art, I am inclined to believe that the highest gift that nature can
give an actor is stage charm.

—Building a Character
—Collected Works, Vol. VIII

See EXHIBITIONISM.

CIRCLE OF ATTENTION

See ATTENTION, PUBLIC SOLITUDE.

CLARITY

[Actions] must be clear like the notes on an instrument . . . otherwise the pattern of movement in a
role is messy, and both its inner and outer rendering
are bound to be indefinite and inartistic. The more
delicate the feeling, the more it requires precision,
clarity and plastic quality in its physical expression.

Clear-cut continuity, finish—these are the hallmarks either of good technique, or of genuine talent. . . . Every moment of the acting of a gifted artist is clear and fully felt.

—*An Actor Prepares*
—*Building a Character*
—*Collected Articles, Speeches, Talks, Letters*

See LOGIC, THROUGH LINE OF ACTION.

CLICHE ACTING

For this there has been worked out a large assortment of picturesque effects which pretend to portray all sorts of feelings through external means. . . . There are special ways of reciting a role . . . with . . . declamatory vocal embellishments . . . for expressing human . . . passions (showing your teeth and rolling the whites of your eyes when you are jealous . . . tearing your hair . . .) of imitating . . . types . . . (peasants spit on the floor . . . aristocrats play with lorgnettes). . . . Some of these established clichés . . . are passed down from generation to generation. . . . They often rush in ahead of feeling and bar the road; that is why an actor must protect himself most conscientiously against such devices and this is true even of gifted actors, capable of true creativeness. . . . The mistake of most actors is that they do not think about the action itself but of its results. . . . Feelings are the result of something that has gone before. . . . As for the result, it will produce itself.

Because of the excitement, the public character of his creative activity, an actor seeks to produce more emotion than he really possesses. . . . He can exag-

gerate his actions, pretending to express feelings . . .
but that destroys them. . . . The protest of his sense
of truth is the best regulator at such times.

—*An Actor Prepares*

See DIRECTOR AS DICTATOR, MECHANICAL ACTING, THE-
ATRICAL EMOTIONS.

COLLECTIVE CREATIVENESS

Every worker in the theatre from the doorman, the
ticket taker, the hat-check girl, to the usher, all the
people the public comes in contact with as they enter
the theatre, on up to the managers, the staff, and finally
the actors themselves—they all are co-creators with
the playwright . . . for the sake of whose play the
audience assembles. They all serve, they are all subject to the fundamental aim of our art. They all, without exception, are participants in the production. Anyone who in any degree obstructs our common effort to
carry out our basic aim should be declared an undesirable member of our community. If any of the staff
out front greets any member of the audience inhos-
pitably, thereby ruining his good humour, he has
struck a blow against . . . the goal of our art. . . .
The playwright, the composer, the cast, all do their
share to create the necessary atmosphere on their side
of the footlights. . . . This absolute dependence of
all the workers in the theatre on the ultimate aim of
our art remains in force not only during performances
but during rehearsals. . . . Artists can operate successfully only under certain necessary conditions. . . .
A bad rehearsal . . . prevents an actor from conveying the thoughts of the playwright, . . . his main job.

If order prevails and the work is properly laid out, teamwork is pleasant and fruitful. . . . Our art is a collective enterprise in which everyone depends on everyone else. . . . It is only in an atmosphere of mutual friendship . . . that talents can thrive.

—*Building a Character*
—*Collected Works, Vol. VI*

See CROWD SCENES, DISCIPLINE, ENSEMBLE, ETHICS IN THE THEATRE.

COMMUNICATION

See ADAPTATION, COMMUNION.

COMMUNION

1. *Communication with the Public Through Your Partner*

If actors really mean to hold the attention of a large audience they must make every effort to maintain an uninterrupted exchange of feelings, thought and actions among themselves, and the inner material for this exchange should be sufficiently interesting to hold spectators.

When you want to communicate with a person you first seek out his soul, his inner world. . . . When you speak to the person who is playing opposite you, learn to follow through until you are certain your thoughts have penetrated his subconsciousness. . . . In turn, you must learn to take in, each time afresh, the words and thoughts of your partner. You must be aware today of his lines even though you have heard them re-peated many times in rehearsals and performances. This connection must be made each time you act to-gether, and this requires a great deal of concentrated attention, technique, and artistic discipline.

Some think that our external, visible movements are a manifestation of activity and that the inner in-visible acts of spiritual communion are not. . . . Every manifestation of inner activity is important and valu-able. Therefore, learn to prize that inner communion because it is one of the important sources of action.

2. *Giving out and Receiving Rays*

Haven't you felt in real life or on the stage, in the course of mutual communion with your partner, that something streamed out of you, some current from your eyes, from the ends of your fingers? . . . What name can we give to these invisible currents which we use to communicate with one another? Some day this phenomenon will be the subject of scientific research. Meantime let us call them *rays*.

The absorbing of those rays is the inverse process. When we are quiescent this process of irradiation is barely perceptible. But when we are in a highly emo-tional state these rays, both given and received, be-come much more definite and tangible.

3. *Grasp*

If you can establish a long, coherent chain of such feelings it will eventually become so powerful that you will have achieved what we call grasp. Then your giv-ing out and absorption [of rays] will be much stronger, keener and more palpable.

We actors must have that same power to seize with our eyes, ears and all our senses. If an actor is to listen.

let him do it intently. . . . If he is to look at something let him really use his eyes. . . . For a simple play you need an ordinary grasp but for a Shakespeare play you have to have an absolute grasp.

[Grasp] is what a bull-dog has in his jaw. . . . But of course this must be done without unnecessary muscular tension.

—An Actor Prepares

See AUDIENCE, CONTACT WITH THE AUDIENCE.

CONCENTRATION

See ATTENTION.

CONTACT WITH THE AUDIENCE

Actors may not maintain contact directly with the audience, but they must do so obliquely. . . . The difficulty is we are in relation with our partner and simultaneously with the spectator. With the former our contact is direct and conscious, with the latter it is indirect and unconscious.

When the spectator is present during . . . an emotional and intellectual exchange, he is like a witness to a conversation, . . . is excited. . . . But the spectators . . . can understand and indirectly participate in what goes on on the stage only while this intercourse continues among the actors.

Speak up, so you will be heard, . . . forget about the public and think only of your acting partners in the play.

—An Actor Prepares

See AUDIENCE, COMMUNION.

CONVENTION

The theatre and its scenery as such is a convention. It cannot be anything else. But does it follow from this that the more of convention there is, the better? Is all convention good and acceptable? There are good and bad conventions; the good may remain, and even be welcome, but the bad should be destroyed. Theatricality is a convention; it is scenic effectiveness in its best sense. All that contributes to the play and the actors' performance should be scenic. The convention that enables the actors to create life in the play and the characters on the stage is good and theatrically effective.

But that life must be convincing. It cannot stem from palpable falseness. Even a lie must assume the aspect of truth to be convincing on the stage; it must seem to possess a truthful quality so that the actors and their audience can believe in this convention.

Good conventions should be beautiful, not just in a theatrically dazzling way. The beautiful is that which uplifts the life of a human being on the stage and in the audience.

The production may be . . . realistic, stylized, modernistic, naturalistic, impressionistic, futuristic—it makes no difference providing it is convincing and true or true-seeming, beautiful in the sense that it is artistic, uplifting, and creative in the sense that it produces the true life of a human spirit without which there can be no art.

Conventions which do not fulfill these requirements are bad.

—*My Life in Art*

See ARTISTIC TRUTH—NATURAL BEAUTY, SENSE OF TRUTH ON THE STAGE.

COPYING

There is the director of exceptional talent who shows the actors how to play their parts. The more gifted his demonstrations, the deeper impression he makes, the greater the actor's enslavement. Having seen the brilliant handling of his part, the actor will wish to play it just as he has seen it demonstrated. He will never be able to get away from the impression he has received, he will be compelled awkwardly to imitate the model. . . . After such a demonstration an actor is shorn of freedom and of his own opinion about his role.

Let every actor produce what he can and not chase after what is beyond his creative powers.

—Creating a Role

See ART OF THE ACTOR AND THE ART OF THE DIRECTOR, DIRECTOR AS DICTATOR, IMITATION.

CORE

See KERNEL OF A PLAY OR PART.

COSTUMES AND ACCESSORIES

When you have created even one role, you know how necessary an actor's wig, beard, costume, props, all are to his creation of an image. . . . Only he who has travelled the difficult path of achieving a physical form for the character he is to play . . . can understand the significance of each detail . . . of make-up and accessories. . . . A costume or an object appropriate to a stage figure ceases to be a simple material thing, it acquires a kind of sanctity for an actor.

One famous actor . . . said that when he was to act in one of his ordinary suits, he would take it off on arriving at the theatre and hang it up. . . . When his make-up was on and it was time for his entrance he would put it on again. . . . But it was no longer an ordinary suit, it was converted into the outer mantle of the character he was playing. . . . This is an important psychological moment . . . and you can tell a true artist by his attitudes towards his costume and properties.

An actor must know how to put on and wear a costume, . . . [he must know] the customs, manners of the times, the ways of greeting people, the use of a fan, sword, cane, hat, handkerchief. . . . He can [only] do all this when he feels himself in his part and his part in himself.

—*Collected Articles, Speeches, Talks, Letters*
—*Collected Works, Vol. III*

See CHARACTERISATION, MAKE-UP, STIMULI TO EMOTION MEMORY.

COUNTERACTION

Every *action* meets with a *reaction* which in turn intensifies the first. In every play, besides the main action we find its opposite counteraction. This is fortunate because its inevitable result is more action. We need that clash of purposes, and all the problems to be solved that grow out of them. They cause activity which is the basis of our art.

—An Actor Prepares

See ACTION.

CREATING THE INNER LIFE OF A ROLE

The fundamental aim of our art is the creation of this life of a human spirit, and its expression in artistic form. That is why we begin by thinking about the inner side of a role and how to create its spiritual life through the internal process of living a part. . . . It is only when an actor feels that his inner and outer life on the stage is flowing naturally and normally . . . that the deeper sources of his subconscious gently open, and from them come feelings. . . . Since we do not understand this governing power . . . we actors call it simply nature. . . . The creative process of living and experiencing a part is an *organic* one, founded on the physical and spiritual laws governing the nature of man.

—An Actor Prepares

See LIVING A PART, NATURE.

CREATIVE INNER STATE

See ELEMENTS OF INNER CREATIVE STATE.

CREATIVE INTENT OF A PLAY

In the production of any significant . . . play, the

director and the actors should strive to arrive at as exact and profound an understanding and grasp of the playwright's creative intent as possible, and not to replace it with any of their own. . . . Actors are in the habit of putting their attention only on the roles assigned to them. . . . This is a mistake. . . . It is very important that they sense the production as a whole, its entire intent. . . . Then, by itself, the part given to you will become clear.

—Collected Works, Vol. VI and VII

See KERNEL OF A PLAY OR A PART, SUPER-OBJECTIVE, THROUGH LINE OF ACTION.

CREATIVE WILL

An actor must have a strong power of will. The first duty of an actor is to learn to control his will. Few actors possess the will and tenacity to do the work which will enable them to achieve true art.

An objective is live bait pursued by our creative will. The bait must be tasty, have substance and the power to charm. Unless it has these qualities it will never attract our attention. The will is ineffectual until it is inspired by some passionate desire. The inspiration for it lies in a fascinating objective. This is a powerful driving force, a strong magnet for our creative will.

—My Life in Art
—Collected Works, Vol. IV

See INNER MOTIVE FORCES, OBJECTIVES.

CRITICS

When I asked a journalist . . . how they produced such remarkable [drama] critics I was told about a very clever and purposeful method used in Germany. They let a young critic write an article full of praise. . . . Anyone could blame . . . but it took a specialist to praise.

The art [of a critic] requires him to have exceptional talent, emotion memory, knowledge and personal qualities. . . . These are rarely united in one person, that is why good critics are so few.

In the first place a critic must be a poet and an artist in order to judge . . . the literary accomplishment of the playwright, and the imaginative creative form given to it by the actor. . . . A critic must be absolutely impartial . . . so that he may inspire confidence in his opinion.

—*My Life in Art*

See CARPING CRITICISM.

CROWD SCENES

The rehearsal of crowd scenes is extraordinarily fatiguing both for the directors and the actors. It is therefore desirable that such rehearsals should be productive but not carried on for long. The strictest discipline must be enforced, everyone must be prepared in advance and well drilled. Every move in a crowd scene is magnified several times over, therefore it must be chosen with greatest care. Unless this is done it cannot be successful.

That is why crowd scenes require all the severity of discipline of a state of martial law. This is not surprising for one director may be handling a mob of several hundred people . . . No one may be late or absent, fail to make notes of the director's instructions, etc.

If there is orderliness and proper distribution of work, your collective effort will be pleasant and productive because it is based on mutual help. . . . You will . . . bear in mind that this is a collective enterprise . . . You are all . . . producing together, you will be helping one another, all be dependent on one another.

There is still another angle in dealing with mob scenes. We are obliged to be in direct, immediate relationship with a mass object. Sometimes we turn to individuals in the crowd; at others we must embrace the whole in a form of extended mutual exchange. The fact that the majority of those making up a mob scene are naturally totally different from one another and that they contribute the most varied emotions and thoughts to this mutual intercourse, very much intensifies the process. Also the group quality excites the temperament of each component member and of all of them together. This excites the principals and that makes a great impression on the spectators.

                                         —An Actor Prepares
                                         —Collected Works, Vol. III

See COMMUNION, DISCIPLINE, ETHICS IN THE THEATRE.

D

DANCE

[The dance] is not a fundamental part of . . . body work. Its role . . . is contributory, preparing us for other important exercises. . . . It is an excellent corrective for the position of arms, legs, backs. . . . Ballet exercises at the bar are . . . splendid. Of equal importance for plasticity and expressiveness of the body is the development of the extremities of the arms and legs, the wrists, fingers, ankles. Learn [from your dancing lessons] to acquire ways of developing, reinforcing and placing your vertebrae. . . . Whereas gymnastics develop motions that are clear-cut to the point of abruptness . . . dancing tends to produce fluency, breadth, cadence in gesture.

—Building a Character

See BALLET, BODY TRAINING, PLASTICITY OF MOTION.

DIRECTOR (RÉGISSEUR)

The responsibility for creating an ensemble, for its artistic integrity, the expressiveness of the over-all performance lies with the director. This applies also to the external shaping of a performance.

We need a régisseur who is a psychologist, an artist. . . . In order to teach others, a régisseur must himself know his subject . . . in the sense that he should to some extent be an actor in his own right. . . . He should himself sense the actors' psycho-technique,

methods and approaches to their parts, all the complicated emotions that are connected with our profession
and with performing in public. Otherwise he will find
no common language with which to speak with them.
The joint work of the director and the actors, the
search for the essential kernel of the play begins with
analysis and proceeds along the line of through-going
action. Later comes the determination of the through
line in each role—that fundamental impetus of each
part which as it derives naturally from its character,
fixes its place in the general action of the play.

This is what the work of a present-day director
should, in my opinion consist of. . . . As for . . . directors, one can only advise them not to foist anything
on their actors, not to tempt them beyond the range of
their capacities, but to enthuse them. . . . Stimulate
in an actor an appetite for his part. This preserves
the freedom of the creative artist.

> —*Collected Works, Vols. VI and VII*
> —*Stanislavski's Legacy*

See ART OF THE ACTOR AND ART OF THE DIRECTOR, DIREC-
TOR AS DICTATOR, ENSEMBLE, REHEARSAL, THEATRE.

DIRECTOR AS DICTATOR

Let us suppose that the director is the strong figure
in the theatre. Then the production plan moves into
first place. The main emphasis is on theatrical effects,
plot, action. There will be much inventiveness, many
stunts, plottings of various kinds and groupings—the
effects will be the important part of the performance.
The role of the actor will be relegated to that of an ac-
cessory, subject to the uses of the director.

In all theatres where the playwright, scene designer or director is paramount, the actor is auxilliary. He is limited to counterfeit characterisation in accordance with the creativeness of others. This leads to cliché acting. With such violent pressure on an actor there can be no question of his truly living his part.

—*Stanislavski's Legacy*

See ART OF THE ACTOR AND ART OF THE DIRECTOR, CLICHÉ ACTING, DIRECTOR (RÉGISSEUR).

DISCIPLINE

An iron discipline . . . is a necessity in any group activity. . . . This applies above all to a complex theatrical performance. . . . Without discipline there can be no theatre art!

—*Building a Character*

See ETHICS IN THE THEATRE.

DOUBLE FUNCTION

[An actor's creative] mood will be unstable at first, until his part is well rounded [out]; and again later, when it gets worn, it loses its keenness.

This wavering back and forth makes it necessary to have a pilot to direct us. As you become more experienced you will find the work of this pilot largely automatic.

Suppose an actor is in perfect possession of his faculties on the stage. His mood is so complete that he can dissect its component parts without getting out of his role. . . . Then there is slight discrepancy. . . . He finds the mistake and corrects it. Yet all the time he can easily continue to play his part even while he is observing himself.

Salvini said: "An actor lives, weeps and laughs on the stage, and all the while he is watching his own tears and smiles. It is this double function, this balance between life and acting that makes his art."

—An Actor Prepares

See INNER CREATIVE STATE.

DRAMA

This is the most difficult subject of study in the art of the theatre. . . . The word itself derives from ancient Greek and contains the meaning of "culminating action." The Latin word "actio" has the root we use in our terms: action, actor, act. Thus drama on the stage is action culminating before our eyes and the actor is a participating element in it.

The art of the theatre has in all times been collective in form and took its rise when the talent of a poet-playwright was active in unison with the talents of actors. . . . The contents of a drama have the character of action unfolding before the eyes of the audience. In it the personalities take their appropriate parts in the action which develops in a consistent and definite direction towards the final goal set by the author. . . . It is only in conjunction with a profound adherence to the artistic individuality of the author, to the ideas and moods which are the creative kernel of the drama, that the theatre can reveal its whole artistic depth and convey the entirety of a poetic work, the graceful form of its composition.

—*An Actor Prepares*
—*Collected Works, Vol. I*
—*My Life in Art*

See COLLECTIVE CREATIVENESS, CREATIVE INTENT, KERNEL OF A PLAY.

E

ELEMENTS OF THE INNER
CREATIVE STATE

We have used the word "elements" to cover artistic talent, qualities, natural gifts and several methods of psycho-techniques. Now we can call them Elements of the Inner Creative State. On the stage, as in real life, the elements—action, objectives, given circumstances, a sense of truth, concentration of attention, emotion memory—should be indivisible. They act simultaneously upon and supplement each other. . . . They are the basic, organic component parts . . . necessary to an actor's creative state.

—An Actor Prepares
—Collected Works, Vol. III

See INNER CREATIVE STATE ON THE STAGE.

EMOTION AND LOGIC

My method is this: I set up a list of actions in which various emotions spontaneously manifest themselves. . . . Take, for example love. What incidents go into the make-up of this human passion? What actions arouse it?

First it was the meeting between "her" and "him." Either immediately, or by degrees . . . the attention of either or both of the future lovers is heightened. They live on the memory of every moment of their meeting. They seek pretexts for another meeting.

There is a second meeting. They have the desire to involve one another in a common interest, common action which will require more frequent meetings, and so on. . . . There is the first secret—an even greater bond to draw them together. They exchange friendly advice about various matters and this makes for constant meetings and communication. So it develops. The first quarrel, reproaches, doubts. Fresh meetings, explanations to dissipate the disagreement. Reconciliation. Still closer relations. Obstacles to their meetings. Secret correspondence. Secret rendezvous. The first present. The first kiss. . . . Growing demands on each other. Jealousy. A break. . . . They meet again. They forgive each other. So it goes on.

All these moments and actions have their inner justification. Taken as a whole they reflect the feelings, the passion, or the state which we describe by the use of the one word *love*.

If you carry out in your imagination—with the right basis of detailed circumstances, proper thinking, sincerity of feeling—each step in this series of actions, you will find that first externally and then internally you will reach the condition of a person in love. With such preparations you will find it easier to take on a role and a play in which this passion figures.

[For] most actors . . . any human passion—love, jealousy, hatred, etc.—is one big and generalized emotion. This is not so.

Every passion is a complex of things experienced emotionally, it is the sum total of a variety of different feelings, experiences, states. All these component parts are not only numerous and varied but they are also often contradictory. In love there is often hatred and scorn, and admiration, and indifference, and ecstacy, and prostration, and embarrassment, and brazenness.

In order to carry out all this, an actor must know the nature of feelings, their logic and continuity.

—Building a Character
—Creating a Role

See LOGIC AND CONTINUITY.

EMOTION MEMORY

That type of memory which makes you relive the sensations you once felt . . . we call *emotion memory*. Just as your visual memory can reconstruct an inner image of some forgotten thing, place or person, your emotion memory can bring back feelings you have already experienced. They may seem beyond recall, when suddenly a suggestion, a thought, a familiar object will bring them back in full force. Sometimes the emotions are as strong as ever, sometimes weaker, sometimes the same strong feelings will come back in a somewhat different guise.

[The Director] made the distinction between sensation memory . . . connected with our five senses, and emotion memory. . . . Sight is the most receptive of impressions. Hearing is also extremely sensitive. . . . Although our senses of smell, taste and touch are useful, and even sometimes important . . . their role is merely auxilliary and for the purpose of influencing our emotion memory.

Time is a splendid filter for our remembered feelings—besides . . . it not only purifies, it also transmutes even painfully realistic memories into poetry.

Your first concern should be to find the means of drawing on your emotional material.

The broader your emotion memory, the richer your material for inner creativeness. . . . It is . . . necessary in addition . . . to distinguish . . . its power, its firmness, the quality of the material it retains. . . . Our whole creative experiences are vivid and full in direct proportion to the power, keenness and exactness of our memory. . . . Sometimes impressions . . . continue to live in us, grow and become deeper. They even stimulate new processes and either fill out unfinished details or suggest altogether new ones.

In time of actual danger a man may remain calm, yet faint away when he recalls the memory of it. This is an example of the increased power of emotion memory over the original feelings experienced.

—An Actor Prepares
—Stanislavski's Legacy

See INNER VISION, MATERIAL FOR CREATIVENESS, REPEATED FEELINGS.

EMPATHY AND FEELING

The emotions of a reader or hearer differ in quality from those of an onlooker or principal. . . . Suppose you were a witness . . . it would be easier to reproduce those feelings. . . . The principal feels [the insult]; the witness can share only sympathetic feelings. But sympathy then might be transformed into direct reaction. . . . The actor may feel the situation of the person in a part so keenly . . . he actually puts himself in the place of that person. . . . In that case the transformation of the emotions of the witness to those of the principal takes place so completely that the strength and quality of the feelings involved are not diminished.

—An Actor Prepares

See ACTORS USE THEIR OWN FEELINGS.

ENSEMBLE

Let us suppose that one actor in a well and carefully prepared production . . . departs so far from the true performance of his part as to act in a purely routine, mechanical way. Has he the right to do this? . . . He was not alone in producing the play, he is not solely responsible for the work put into it. In such an enterprise one works for all and all for one. There must be mutual responsibility. . . . In spite of my great admiration for individual splendid talents, I do not accept the star system; collective creative effort is the root of our kind of art. That requires ensemble acting and whoever mars that ensemble is committing a crime . . . against the very art he serves. The public like us in plays, where we have a clear-cut . . . *superobjective* and a well executed *through line of action.* . . . That includes everything: ensemble acting, good actors and a proper understanding of the play produced.

—Collected Articles, Speeches, Talks, Letters
—Collected Works, Vol. III

See CROWD SCENES, DISCIPLINE, ETHICS IN THE THEATRE, SUPER-OBJECTIVE.

ETHICS IN THE THEATRE

One more element . . . contributing to a creative dramatic state . . . I shall call . . . ethics. [The actor] needs order, discipline, a code of ethics not only for the general circumstances of his work, but also and especially for his artistic . . . purposes. . . . An actor . . . always being in the public eye displaying his best aspects, receiving ovations, accepting extravagant praise, reading glowing criticisms—all . . . these breed . . . the sense of craving for constant titillation of his personal vanity. But if he lives only on that he is bound to sink low and become trivial. A serious-minded person could not be entertained long by such a life, yet a shallow one is enthralled, debauched, destroyed by it. That is why in our world of the theatre we must learn to hold ourselves well in check . . . follow the principle: Love art in yourself, and not yourself in art.

—Building a Character

See DISCIPLINE.

EXHIBITIONISM

There are actors . . . who are in love with themselves, who always . . . show, not images and creations, but themselves. . . . They need Romeo and Hamlet [to play] only as a frivolous girl needs a new dress. Many [actors] use their lines as a vehicle to exhibit some vocal attributes, diction, manner of recitation, the technique of their own voice production.

We know of many cases when [stage charm] has brought ruin to an actor because . . . he devoted all

his interest and technical equipment to the sole purpose of self-exhibition.

It is almost as though nature revenges herself on an
actor for his inability to make the right use of her
gifts, because self-admiration and exhibitionism impair and destroy the power of charm. The actor becomes the victim of his own splendid, innate endowment.

—Building a Character
—My Life in Art

See CHARM.

EXPLOITERS OF ART

The theatre, on account of its publicity and spec-
tacular side, attracts many people who merely want to
capitalize their beauty or make careers. They take advantage of the ignorance of the public, its perverted
taste, favouritism, intrigues, false success, and many
other means which have no relation to creative art.
These exploiters are the deadliest enemies of art.

—An Actor Prepares

See EXHIBITIONISM.

EXTERNAL TECHNIQUE

An actor is under the obligation to live his part inwardly, and then to give this experience an external
embodiment . . . in a beautiful, artistic form. . . .
The dependence of the body on the soul is particularly
important in our school of art. . . . In order to express a most delicate and largely subconscious life, it is

necessary to have control of an unusually responsive, excellently prepared vocal and physical apparatus. . . . That is why an actor of our type is obliged to work so much more than others . . . on his outer physical apparatus.

When the body transmits neither the actor's feelings to me nor how he experiences them, I see an out-of-tune, inferior instrument . . . on which a fine musician is obliged to perform. . . . The more complex the life of the human spirit in the part being portrayed, the more delicate, the more compelling and artistic should be the physical form which clothes it. . . . This makes an enormous call on our external technique, on the expressiveness of our bodily apparatus, our voice, diction, intonation, handling of words, phrases, speeches, our facial expression, plasticity of movement, way of walking. . . . You must still go on developing, correcting, tuning your bodies until every part of them will respond to the . . . complex task . . . of presenting in external form your invisible feelings. What classic part can you hope to play, if you do not possess an adequately trained physical apparatus? . . . You may have inside you a magnificent line [of feelings] but you will not be able to produce them on the stage. You cannot play Bach or Beethoven beautifully on an untuned instrument, . . . nor sing an opera with an untrained voice.

—*An Actor Prepares*
—*Building a Character*

See BODY TRAINING, CHARACTERISATION AND TRANSFORMATION, PLASTICITY OF MOTION, SPEECH, WALKING ON THE STAGE.

EYES

How often we actors stand on the stage and see nothing! Yet what can be more awful than an actor with vacant eyes? They are such obvious evidence of the fact that the soul of the actor playing the role is dormant . . . or otherwise engaged in matters unrelated to his role.

A chattering tongue or mechanically moving hands cannot take the place of the comprehending eye. The eye of an actor which looks at and sees an object attracts the attention of the spectator, and by the same token points out to him what he should look at. Conversely, a blank eye lets the attention of the spectator wander away from the stage.

There exist formal, truthful and so to say "legitimate" ways of using a vacant stare.

I need not tell you . . . that the eye is the mirror of the soul. The vacant eye is the mirror of the empty soul. . . . You must learn how to show your eyes to a crowd made up of thousands of spectators. Across the huge space of an auditorium it is not easy to distinguish those two small dots which are your eyes. For a spectator to be able to do this the actor must be able to sustain his look and the object he is looking at must not move. Although turns and movements are possible, they must be effected in relation to the expression of the eyes and the face. You must regulate your activity so that your eyes can be seen.

—*An Actor Prepares*
—*Collected Works, Vol. II*

See AUDIENCE, COMMUNION, CONTACT WITH THE AUDIENCE.

F

FACE

Facial expressions are brought about of their own accord, naturally, as a result of intuition, inner feelings. Nevertheless their effectiveness can improve through the exercise and development of flexibility of facial muscles. Yet . . . to accomplish this one must be familiar with the muscular anatomy of the face.

An actor must work out a conscious control of all groups of muscles and the capacity to sense the energy flowing along them . . . for the definite purpose of forming his facial expressiveness, gestures, etc.

—Collected Works, Vols. III and VI

See EXTERNAL TECHNIQUE, GESTURE, TUMBLING.

FAITH

An actor must above all believe in what is happening around him . . . [and] in what he himself is doing. . . . From the instant when he is transported from the plane of actuality to that of an imagined life and believes in it, he can begin to create. We can use ordinary chairs to outline anything the imagination of an author, or director can ask us to create: horses, city squares, ships, forests. It will do no harm if we find ourselves unable to believe that this chair is a particular object because even without the belief we may have the feeling it arouses.

Truth on the stage is whatever we can believe in

with sincerity, whether in ourselves or in our colleagues. Truth cannot be separated from belief, nor belief from truth . . . and without both of them it is impossible to live your part, or to create anything. Believe in what you yourself say or do on the stage and you will be convincing.

> —*An Actor Prepares*
> —*Collected Works, Vol. I, II and III*

See SENSE OF TRUTH ON THE STAGE, SINCERITY OF EMOTIONS.

FANTASY

Imagination creates things that can be or can happen, whereas fantasy invents things that are not in existence, which never have been or will be. . . . Both fantasy and imagination are indispensable.

Science, literature, painting . . . only hint . . . at imaginary flights into the realm of the non-existent. In dreaming about this the major creative work is done by our fantasy. And here it is more necessary than ever to make use of means to draw what is fantastic closer to what is real: logic and continuity. . . . They help to make the impossible more probable.

> —*An Actor Prepares*

See IMAGINATION, LOGIC AND CONTINUITY.

FENCING

See BODY TRAINING.

FINGERS

If the eyes are the mirror of the soul, then the tips of the fingers are the eyes of our body.

Your hands are not reflecting any truthful meaning when they are not developed. You must learn to feel . . . with the tips of your fingers. Even the slightest tenseness there will keep you from entering the realm of the subconscious. Develop your wrists and hands. Spend a whole week on them, then check up on and keep nagging each other.

Of course hands can assume twenty thousand different positions, but you should know how to provide a justifiable basis for each one. . . . The main thing is to have free fingers, then they will fall into the right place . . . develop extraordinary lightness. In every role he sang Chaliapin had different hands.

—An Actor Prepares
—Talks with Opera Studio Students, 1935

See BALLET, EYES, RELAXATION OF MUSCLES.

FINISH

See CLARITY, RESTRAINT IN GESTURES.

FIRST ACQUAINTANCE WITH A PLAY

As important an event as your acquaintance with the work of a poet, . . . this moment of your first meeting with a part should be unforgettable. . . . I attribute decisive significance to these first impressions. If the impressions are properly received, that is a great gauge of future success. The loss of this moment is irreparable because a second reading no longer contains the element of surprise so potent in the realm of intuitive creativeness. To correct a spoiled impression is more difficult than to create a proper one in the first place. *One must be extraordinarily attentive to one's first acquaintance with a part because this is the first stage of creativeness.*

—*Creating a Role*

See ROLE INSIDE THE ACTOR.

G

GENIUS

To a genius the creative inner state is almost always naturally available, in highest and fullest degree. . . . The greater the simplicity with which one approaches a genius, the more accessible and intelligible he becomes. A genius must be simple, that is one of his greatest merits.

—Collected Works, Vol. VII
—My Life in Art

See ELEMENTS OF THE INNER CREATIVE STATE.

GESTURE

A gesture made for its own sake has no place on the stage. . . . We have no use for ballet methods, for theatrical poses or gestures which are superficial in origin. They cannot convey the life of a human spirit.

We would do better to adapt these theatrical conventions, poses, gestures to the execution of some live objective, to the expression of some inner experience. Then a gesture ceases to be merely a gesture and is converted into a genuine, meaningful and purposeful action. . . . Superfluous gestures are the same as trash, dirt, spots. . . . *Let every actor above all hold his gestures in check to the extent that he controls them and not they him.*

A gesture by itself which does not carry out some action germane to a role, has no purpose on the stage, except in a few rare instances where it is related to a character part. No [conventional] gesture can convey the inner life of a role, nor promote its through line of action. For that purpose movements which create physical activity are needed.

On the stage I reject any unmotivated gesture, I accept only *action*, movement.

—*Building a Character*
—*Collected Works, Vol. VIII*

See RESTRAINT IN GESTURES.

GIVEN CIRCUMSTANCES

This expression means . . . the story of the play, the facts, events, epoch, time and place of action, conditions of life, the actors' and régisseur's (director's) interpretation, the mise-en-scène, the production, the sets, the costumes, properties, lighting and sound effects—all the circumstances that are given to an actor to take into account as he creates his role.

[The *Magic*] *If* is the starting point, the given circumstances, the development.

—*An Actor Prepares*

See ANALYSIS, APPRAISING THE FACTS OF A PLAY, APHORISM OF PUSHKIN.

GROTESQUE

You say Pushkin must be played quite differently, more fully, the way he wrote, otherwise the images he created tend to become shallow to the point of turning into simple, national types of historic figures, and therefore Pushkin can be presented only in tragic grotesque [style], as Molière can be in tragicomic grotesque. . . . Now we shall examine the grotesque only from your point of view. . . . Did you ever in your life see this kind of grotesque? I saw one example of it. It was the Othello of Salvini. And I also saw a comic grotesque or, to be exact, actors capable of creating it. These were old Zhivokini and Varlamov.

Genuine grotesque is a vivid and bold externalization based on such tremendous all-embracing inner content that reaches the limits of exaggeration. An actor must not only feel and experience human passions in all their universal, component elements—he must over and above this condense them and produce a manifestation of them so vivid, so irresistible in its expressiveness, so audacious, so bold that it borders on the burlesque. The grotesque may not be unintelligible, there can be no question mark placed after it. The grotesque must be definite and clear to the point of brazenness. It would be too bad if any spectator, after seeing your grotesque, should ask: "Tell me, please, what is the meaning of those four crooked eyebrows and the black triangle on the cheek of Pushkin's Miser Knight or Salieri?" It would be too bad if after that you had to explain: "Well, you see the artist wanted to picture a sharp eye, and since symmetry is soothing he introduced that slant. . . ." There lies the grave of the grotesque. It dies and in its place is born a simple riddle, as silly and naïve as the ones they publish in the illustrated magazines. . . . What do I care how many eyebrows or noses an actor has? Let him have four eyebrows, two noses, a dozen eyes. But they must be justified by the fact that the actor's inner content is so great that two eyebrows, one nose, two eyes are not enough for him to project all this immense spiritual content. But if the four eyebrows are not based on necessity, if théy have no justifiable basis, such grotesque makes the actor smaller, it does not inflate his little being. To inflate something which is non-existent, to inflate emptiness—that makes me think of blowing soap bubbles. . . . When the form is greater and more powerful than the actual being . . . that is grotesque. . . . Yet is it worth while breaking our hearts about something which, alas, practically does not exist, something we see only in the rarest, exceptional instances in our art? To tell the truth, have you ever seen a stage creation of such all-embracing content that imperatively called for the enlarged and exaggerated form of the grotesque in which to be expressed? . . . How often one does see a great blown-up form, inflated like a soap bubble, to the point of external, make-believe grotesque, but completely lacking in all content! You must realize that this is just a pie with nothing inside, a bottle without wine, a body without a soul. . . . Such grotesque without spiritual motive or content . . . is mere affectation.

The pseudo-grotesque is the worst, and the genuine grotesque is the best kind of art. . . . The pseudo-grotesque is not characterisation and the genuine grotesque is greater than simple characterisation. It is not a partial art but a whole art carried to the point of an all-embracing, universal manifestation of the thing created. The true grotesque is the ideal of our theatre creativity.

—*Collected Works, Vol. IV*
—*Stanislavski's Legacy*

See SYMBOLISM.

H

HABITS

Habit is a two-edged sword. It can do great harm when badly used on the stage and be of great value when proper advantage is taken of it.

It is essential . . . to establish the right creative state by forming trained habits.

The unfortunate and dangerous part . . . is that habits can be developed in the wrong direction. The more often an actor appears on the stage and acts in a theatrical, untrue way and not according to the true dictates of his nature, the farther he will move away from the goal we seek to achieve.

It is essential to work . . . step by step when you are learning to establish . . . trained habits. . . . Piecemeal the system enters the . . . actor, until it . . . becomes incorporated in his own second nature. "The difficult should become habitual, the habitual easy, the easy, beautiful" (quoted from S. M. Volkonski).

— *Building a Character*

See DISCIPLINE.

HERE AND NOW

It is extremely important to an actor's creative state to feel what we call "I am." I exist here and now as part of the life of a play, on the stage. . . . To help an actor *find himself in his role and the role in himself*

. . . let him decide sincerely how to answer the question: What would I do here and now, if in real life I had to act under circumstances analogous to those in which my part is set?

—*Collected Works, Vol. III*

See "I AM," INNER CREATIVE STATE ON THE STAGE, MAGIC IF, ROLE INSIDE THE ACTOR.

HIGH-TENSION ACTING

Different actors have different conceptions of effect through speech. Some of them try to find it in physical tension. They clench their fists, they heave . . . make themselves shake from head to foot, all for the sake of impressing the public. Under that method the voice is pressed out . . . in a horizontal line. . . . This . . . is . . . what we call "high-tension" acting. Actually it does not produce volume; it leads only to shouting, to hoarseness with a narrowed vocal range.

—*Building a Character*

See CONTACT WITH THE AUDIENCE, VOICE VOLUME.

HOME-WORK

For an actor, more than for an artist in other fields, work at home is indispensable.

Whereas a singer has to be concerned only with his voice and breathing, a dancer with his physical apparatus, and a pianist with his hands or a wind instrumentalist with his breathing and lip technique—an actor is responsible [at one and the same time] for his arms, his legs, his eyes, his face, the plasticity of his

whole body, his rhythm, his motion, *and* all the pro-
gramme of our activities here in school. These exercises . . . go on through your whole lives as artists.
The great majority of actors are convinced that they
need to work only at rehearsals and that at home they
can enjoy their leisure. But this is not so. In rehearsals
an actor merely clarifies the work he should be doing
at home. At home an actor should do work on himself
to correct shortcomings which have been pointed out
to him by his instructor.

—Building a Character

See PLASTICITY OF MOVEMENT, VOICE.

I

"I AM"

In our theatre parlance this means that I have put myself into the very centre of imaginary circumstances, . . . that I exist at the heart of an imaginary life, in a world of imaginary things, . . . and that I am on the point of going into action . . . on my own responsibility.

As a participant . . . you cannot see yourself, but only what surrounds you. . . . You react with your inner nature to what is going on as truly as in real life.

If you sense the truth in a play subconsciously, your faith in it will naturally follow, and the state of "I am." . . . The smallest action or sensation, the slightest technical means, can acquire a deep significance . . . only if it is pushed to its limit of possibility, to the boundary of human *truth,* faith and the sense of "I am." When this point is reached, your whole spiritual and physical make-up will function normally.

—*Collected Works, Vol. II*

See FAITH, HERE AND NOW, SENSE OF TRUTH ON THE STAGE.

IDEAL ARTIST

Imagine some *ideal artist* who has decided to devote himself to a single, large purpose in life; to elevate and entertain the public by a high form of art; to expound the hidden, spiritual beauties in the writings of poetic geniuses. . . . His whole life will be consecrated to this high cultural mission.

Another type of artist may use his personal success to convey his own ideas and feelings to the masses. Great people may have a variety of high purposes.

In their cases the super-objective of any one production will be merely a step in the fulfillment of an important life purpose, . . . a *supreme-objective*.

—An Actor Prepares

IDENTIFICATION

See ANALYSIS, CHARACTERIZATION.

IMAGINARY OBJECTS

When you reach the point of playing Hamlet, threading a way through his intricate psychology to the moment when he kills the King, will it be important for you to have a life-size sword in your hand? If you lack one, will you be unable to finish your performance? You can kill the King without a sword and you can light a fire without matches. What needs to burn is your imagination.

[In] communion with an imaginary, unreal, non-existent object, such as an apparition . . . some people try to delude themselves into thinking that they really see it. They exhaust all their energy and attention on such an effort. But an experienced actor knows that the point does not lie in the apparition itself, but in his inner relation to it. Therefore he tries to give an honest answer to his own question: What should I do if a ghost appeared before me?

—An Actor Prepares

See COMMUNION, IMAGINATION.

IMAGINATION

Imagination creates things that can be or can happen. . . . *Every movement you make on the stage, every word you speak, is the result of the right life of your imagination.*

The creative process starts with the imaginative invention of a poet, a writer, the director of the play, the actor, the scene designer, and others in the production, so the first in order should be *imagination*.

If imagination plays such an important part in an actor's work, what can he do if he lacks it? He must develop it or else leave the stage. . . . It all depends on what kind of an imagination you have. . . . The kind that has initiative . . . will work . . . untiringly, whether you are awake or asleep. Then there is the kind that lacks initiative, but is easily aroused. . . . Observation of the nature of gifted people does disclose to us a way to control the emotion needed in a part. This way lies through the action of the imagination which to a far greater degree is subject to the effect of conscious will. We cannot directly act on our emotions, but we can prod our creative fantasy and [it] stirs up our *emotion* or *affective memory*, calling up from its secret depths, beyond the reach of consciousness, elements of already experienced emotions, and re-groups them to correspond with the images which arise in us. . . . That is why a creative fantasy is a fundamental, absolutely necessary gift for an actor.

There are various aspects of the life of the imagination. . . . We can use our inner eye to see all sorts of visual images, living creatures, human faces, their features, landscapes, the material world of objects, settings and so forth. With our inner ear we can hear all sorts of melodies, voices, intonations and so forth. We can feel things in imagination at the prompting of our sensation and emotion memory.

There are actors of things seen and actors of things heard. The first are gifted with an especially fine inner vision and the second with sensitive inner hearing. For the first type, to which I myself belong, the easiest way to create an imaginary life is with the help of visual images. For the second type it is the image of sound that helps.

We can cherish all these visual, audible, or other images; we can enjoy them passively . . . be the audience of our own dreams. Or we can take an *active* part in those dreams.

Every invention of the actor's imagination must be thoroughly worked out. . . . It must be able to answer all the questions (when, where, why, how) that he asks himself when he is driving his inventive faculties on to make a more and more definite picture of a make-believe existence.

[*The actor*] *must feel the challenge physically as well as intellectually* because the imagination . . . can reflexively affect our physical nature and make it act. . . . Not a step should be taken on the stage without the cooperation of your imagination.

—*An Actor Prepares*
—*Building a Character*
—*Creating a Role*
—*Stanislavski's Legacy*

See EMOTION MEMORY, FANTASY, INNER VISION.

IMITATING

See COPYING.

IMITATION

In my . . . admiration for a great actor I attempted to imitate him. . . . This has its good and its bad side: copying a great example can train you in a good pattern, but it also checks your individual creativeness. . . . I was only repeating what the other person had experienced in his emotions. . . . Since my imitation was purely external . . . I strained myself physically to produce feelings. . . . Finally I realized the simple truth that such an approach to a part . . . can never produce the image [of a character].

—*My Life in Art*

See LIVING A PART.

IMMOBILITY

I had thought that immobility . . . would allow me to devote all my energy and attention to the inner life of my role. As it turned out this arbitrary immobility which was not based on any inner necessity . . . gave rise to extreme tension and tautness of body and soul. . . . This was quite understandable; faced with this arbitrary forcing of nature all feeling evaporated and was replaced by mechanical, cliché acting.

The actor, who is obliged to remain seated throughout an entire performance, must of necessity assure his right to this immobility vis à vis an audience of thousands who have come to the theatre to look at him. He can only justify remaining immobile by the inner activity of his spirit as dictated by the psychological pattern of his role.

—*Collected Works, Vol. I*
—*My Life in Art*

See ACTION, INNER TENSION, JUSTIFICATION, RELAXATION OF MUSCLES.

IMPROVISATION

When teaching is oriented toward a practical and even interesting objective it is easier to convince and influence students. . . . Our point of departure in training actors is to have them learn by acting [improvisations]. . . . One cannot go on teaching for years in a classroom and only at the end ask a student to act. In that space of time he will have lost all creative faculty. . . . Creativeness must never cease, the only question being the choice of material on which to base it. . . . In our kind of acting we make frequent use of improvisations. . . . This kind of creativeness gives a freshness and an immediacy to a performance.

In the beginning it is best to take subjects which are within your reach, and not too overburdened with complicated psychology . . . but even the most primary kind of exercises must be carried to the point of mastery, of virtuosity in execution. It is not the job of teachers to give instruction in how to create, we should only push students in the right direction, while training their taste, requiring from them the observance of the laws of nature, and the execution of their simplest exercises carried to the point of art, which is to say absolute truthfulness and technical perfection.

Improvisations which they work out themselves are an excellent way to develop the imagination. . . . Student actors who have been trained on improvisations later on find it easy to use their imaginative fancy on a play where this is needed.

In addition to the development of imagination improvisations . . . have another asset: while working on one an actor naturally, without even perceiving it, learns the creative laws of organic nature and the methods of psycho-technique.

—*Collected Works, Vol. III*
—*Year Book of the Moscow Art Theatre, 1947*

See IMAGINATION, NATURE, PSYCHO-TECHNIQUE.

INNER ARDOUR

Anything you do on the stage with coldness inside you will destroy you because it will encourage in you the habit of automatic, mechanical action, without imagination.

What can be more effective, fan your ardour, excite you inwardly, than an imaginary fiction which has taken possession of you?

A true artist is on fire with what he sees going on all around him, he is ardently interested in life, it becomes for him the object of his study and his passions. . . . He tries to record the impressions he receives from the outside, and as an artist . . . stamp them on his heart. . . . One cannot be cold when working in art. . . . You have to possess a certain degree of inner warmth.

Our mind can be set to work at any time. But it is not sufficient. We must have the ardent and direct cooperation of our emotions, desires, and all the other elements of our inner creative state. . . . Just as yeast causes fermentation, so the sensing of the life of his role imparts a kind of inner warmth, the ebullition necessary to the actor.

Artistic enthusiasm is a motive power in creativeness. Excited fascination which accompanies enthusiasm is a subtle critic, an incisive inquirer, and the best guide into the depths of feeling which are unattainable to a conscious approach.

The ability to fire his feelings, his will, and his mind —that is one of the qualities of an actor's talent, one of the principal objectives of his inner technique.

—An Actor Prepares
—Creating a Role

See INNER MOTIVE FORCES.

INNER CONTENT

See ACTION.

INNER CREATIVE STATE ON THE STAGE

When an actor comes out on the stage before an audience he may lose his self-possession from fright, embarrassment . . . [or] a sense of overwhelming responsibility. . . . At that moment he is incapable of speaking, listening . . . thinking, feeling . . . , or even moving in an ordinary human way. He feels a nervous need to gratify the public, to show himself and to hide his own state . . . (which we call a mechanical, theatrical mood) .

I clearly realized the harm inherent in the mechanical, theatrical mood, so I began to search for some other spiritual and physical state while on the stage which would be beneficial rather than harmful to the creative process. . . . My observations taught me . . . that in the creative state a large role is played by the absence of all physical tension, the complete subordination of the body to the actor's will. . . . Then I perceived that creativeness is first of all conditioned by the complete concentration of an actor's entire nature.

So an actor turns to his spiritual and physical creative instrument. His mind, will and feelings combine to mobilize all of his inner "elements." . . . Out of this fusion of elements arises an important inner state . . . the inner creative mood. The habit of being daily on the stage and in the right creative state is what produces actors who are masters of their art.

—An Actor Prepares
—My Life in Art

See ATTENTION, ELEMENTS OF THE INNER CREATIVE STATE, PUBLIC SOLITUDE, TALENT.

INNER IMAGES AND HEARING

As long as we are acting creatively this film (an unbroken series of images) will be thrown on the screen of our inner vision, making vivid the circumstances among which we are moving. . . .

As to these inner images, . . . is it correct to say we feel them inside of us? We possess the faculty to see things which are not there by making a mental picture of them.

This inner stream of images . . . is a great help to the actor in fixing his attention on the inner life of his part.

The same process occurs when we are dealing with sounds. We hear imaginary noises with an inner ear.

—An Actor Prepares

See IMAGINATION, INNER VISION.

INNER LIFE OF A ROLE

See APPRAISING THE FACTS OF A PLAY.

INNER MOTIVE FORCES

The first, and most important master [is] *feeling* . . . unfortunately it is not tractable. . . . Since you cannot begin your work unless your feelings happen to function of their own accord, it is necessary for you to have recourse to some other master. . . . Who is it? The second master is the *mind*. . . . Your mind can be a motive power in . . . your creative process. Is there a third? . . . If longings could put your creative apparatus to work and direct it spiritually . . . we have found our third master—*will*. Consequently we have three impelling movers in our psychic life.

Since these three forces form a triumvirate, inextricably bound up together, what you say of the one necessarily concerns the other two. . . . This combined power is of utmost importance to us actors and we should be gravely mistaken not to use it for our practical ends. . . . Actors whose feelings over-balance their intellects will, naturally, in playing Romeo or Othello, emphasize the emotional side. Actors in whom the will is the most powerful attribute will play Macbeth or Brand and underscore ambition, or fanaticism. The third type will unconsciously stress, more than is necessary, the intellectual shadings of a part like Hamlet or Nathan the Wise.

It is, however, necessary not to allow any one of the three elements to crush out either of the others and thereby upset the balance and necessary harmony. Our

art recognizes all three types and in their creative work
all three forces play leading parts.

—An Actor Prepares

See CREATIVE WILL.

INNER TENSION

In our inner being there are many superfluous tensions. But it is necessary to handle these inner tensions
in quite a different way and not as we deal with plain
muscles. Inner elements are like cobwebs in compari-
son with muscles which are more like cables. Separate
cobwebs can easily be broken up, but if you plait them
together into ropes you will not be able to cut them
with an axe. So be careful how you handle them in
their incipient state. . . . There are three stages in
them too: tension, release, justification. In the first two
stages you seek out the severest inner tension, identify
what causes it and try to destroy it. In the third stage
you justify your new inner state on the basis of appropriate given circumstances.

—Collected Works, Vol. II

See PUBLIC SOLITUDE, RELAXATION OF MUSCLES.

INNER TONE

See SCORE OF A ROLE.

INNER VISION

Inner images are formed inside of us, in our imagina-
tions, our memories and then, as it were, we externalize
them, so that we may examine them. Yet we look at

these imagined objects, so to say, from the inside, not with our external, but with our inner eyes.

I may also say, to turn the phrase around, that although these imaginary objects and images are suggested to us by outside life they nevertheless are first shaped within us, in our imagination and memory.

It is only against the background of such explanations that we can accept the term "inner vision."

—*An Actor Prepares*
—*Collected Works, Vol. II*

See IMAGINARY OBJECTS, IMAGINATION, INNER IMAGES.

INSPIRATION

The most important [difficulty] is the abnormal circumstance of an actor's creative work. . . . Other [non-performing] artists can create when they are under the influence of inspiration. But an actor himself is obliged to call forth his inspiration at the exact time he is advertised to come out and perform. . . . The very best that can happen is to have the actor completely carried away by the play; then regardless of his own will he lives the part . . . subconsciously and with inspiration. No such genius exists. . . . Therefore our art teaches us first of all to create consciously . . . because that will best prepare the way for . . . inspiration. Realism, and even naturalism, in the inner preparation of a part is essential, because it causes your subconscious to work and induces outbursts of inspiration. . . . We need a creative . . . subconscious and the place to look for it above all is in a stirring objective. . . . When an actor is completely absorbed by some profoundly moving objective, so that he throws his whole being passionately into its execution, he reaches a state we call *inspiration*.

If today you are in good form and are blessed with inspiration, forget about technique and abandon yourself to your feelings. But an actor should remember that inspirations appear only on holidays. Therefore there must be some other well-prepared course for him to follow and which he can control. . . . The easiest one for him to establish is the line of physical actions. . . . Let him absorb all the technical means at his disposal until they become second nature. Let him adopt the given circumstances of his part so completely that they become his very own. Only then may his ultrasensitive inspiration decide . . . to emerge, and take into her power and direction his creative initiative.

Give up chasing this phantom, inspiration. Leave it to that miraculous fairy nature.

—An Actor Prepares

See ADAPTATIONS, "INSPIRATION" ACTORS, NATURE, PSYCHO-TECHNIQUE, SUBCONSCIOUS, TALENT.

"INSPIRATION" ACTORS

There are individual moments when you suddenly and unexpectedly rise to great artistic heights and thrill your audience. In such moments you are creating according to your inspiration . . . but would you feel yourself capable enough to play five great acts of *Othello* with the same lift with which you accidentally played part of that one short scene? . . . Such an undertaking would be far beyond the strength of a genius with an extraordinary temperament. . . . For our purposes you must have . . . a well worked-out psychological technique, an enormous talent, and great physical and nervous reserves. You have not all these things any more than the "inspiration" actors who do not admit technique. They, as you did, rely entirely on inspiration. If this inspiration does not turn up, neither you nor they have anything with which to fill in the blank spaces.

Almost as a rule actors do not admit that laws, techniques, theories, much less a system, have any part in their work. Actors are overwhelmed by their "genius" in quotation marks. The less gifted the actor the greater his "genius" and it doesn't allow him to make any conscious approach to his art. Such actors . . . believe that any conscious factor in creativeness is only a nuisance. They find it easier to be an actor by the grace of God. I shall not deny that there are times when, for unknown reasons, they are able to have an intuitive, emotional hold on their parts and they play reasonably well in a scene or even in a whole performance. But an actor cannot gamble his career on a few accidental successes. . . . Accident is not art. . . . You cannot build on it.

—*An Actor Prepares*
—*Building a Character*

See AMATEUR ATTITUDE, INSPIRATION.

INTONATIONS AND PUNCTUATION

Punctuation signs require special vocal intonations. . . . Without these intonations they do not fulfill their functions. . . . In each of these intonations there is a certain effect; the exclamation sign for sympathy, approval or protest; a colon demands attentive consideration for what follows, and so on. There is great expressiveness in all these [signs]. The external word, by means of intonation, affects one's emotion memory, feelings. . . . Take the comma. . . . It possesses a miraculous quality. Its curve . . . causes listeners to wait patiently for the end of the unfinished sentence. . . . Intonations and pauses in themselves possess the power to produce . . . an emotional effect.

—Building a Character

See ACCENTUATION, PAUSES IN SPEECH, SPEECH, VOICE VOLUME.

INTUITION

See CHARACTERISATION AND TRANSFORMATION, NATURE, PSYCHO-TECHNIQUE, SUBCONSCIOUS.

J

JUSTIFICATION

Put life into all the imagined circumstances and actions until you have completely satisfied your sense of truth and until you have awakened a sense of faith in the reality of your sensations. This . . . is what we call justification of a part. What difference is there . . . between the dry catalogue of facts as read . . . when I first became acquainted with the play, and the present appraisal of those same facts? . . . Now they are living events in an infinitely exciting day, impregnated with life, indeed my own.

—An Actor Prepares
—Creating a Role

See ACTORS USE THEIR OWN FEELINGS, APPRAISING THE FACTS OF A PLAY.

K

KERNEL OF A PLAY OR PART

The aim of a theatre should be to create the inner life of a play and its physical embodiment on the stage in consonance with the essential kernel and idea which gave birth to the work of the playwright.

The problem for our art and consequently for our theatre is—to create an inner life for a play and its characters, to express in physical and dramatic terms the fundamental core, the idea which impelled the writer, the poet to produce his composition.

—Building a Character

See SUPER-OBJECTIVE, THROUGH LINE OF ACTION.

L

LIMITATIONS

Some actors do not fully realize the limitations placed on them by nature. They undertake problems beyond their powers to solve. The comedian wants to play tragedy, the old man to be a *jeune premier*, the simple type longs for heroic parts and the soubrette for the dramatic. This can only result in forcing, impotence, and stereotyped, mechanical action. These are shackles and your only means of getting out of them is to study your art and yourself in relation to it.

—*An Actor Prepares*

See CHARACTERISATION AND TRANSFORMATION, EXTERNAL TECHNIQUE, NATURE, TYPES.

LINE OF PHYSICAL BEING

See ACTION, EXTERNAL TECHNIQUE.

LIVING A PART

The approach we have chosen—the art of living a part—[asserts] that the main factor in any form of creativeness is the life of a human spirit, that of the actor and his part, their joint feelings and subconscious creation. . . . What we hold in highest regard are impressions made on our emotions, which leave a lifelong mark on the spectator and transform actors into real, living beings. . . . Aside from the fact that it opens up avenues for inspiration, living a part helps the artist to carry out one of his main objectives. His job is not to present merely the external life of his character. He must fit his own human qualities to the life of this other person, and pour into it all of his own soul. . . . An artist takes the best that is in him and carries it over on the stage. The form will vary according to the necessities of the play, but the human emotions of the artist will remain alive, and they cannot be replaced by anything else.

Therefore, no matter how much you act, how many parts you take, you should never allow yourself any exception to the rule of using your own feelings.

Salvini said: "The great actor . . . should feel the thing he is portraying . . . not only once or twice while he is studying his part, but to a greater or lesser degree every time he plays it, no matter whether it is the first or thousandth time."

Always act in your own person. . . . You can never get away from yourself. The moment you lose yourself on the stage marks the departure from truly living your part and the beginning of exaggerated, false acting.

Spiritual realism, truth of artistic feelings . . . these are the most difficult (achievements) of our art, they require long, arduous inner preparation.

The difference between my art and that [practiced by others] is the difference between "seeming" and "being."

—An Actor Prepares
—Building a Character

See ACTORS USE THEIR OWN FEELINGS, PSYCHO-TECHNIQUE, WHAT IS MY SYSTEM?

LIVING IMAGE

Each dramatic and artistic image, created on the stage, is unique and cannot be repeated, just as in nature.

Without an external form neither your inner characterisation, nor the spirit of your image will reach the public. The external characterisation explains and illustrates.

An actor is called upon to create an image while he is on the stage and not just show himself off to the public. . . . All actors who are artists, creators of images, should make use of characterisation.

There are some actors, for whom the image they have created becomes their alter ego, their double. The image never leaves them. . . . They constantly watch the image, not in order to copy it, but because they find themselves under its spell, in its power, and they act thus or thus because they are living the life of their image.

—An Actor Prepares
—Building a Character

See CHARACTERISATION AND TRANSFORMATION, EXTERNAL TECHNIQUE.

LOGIC AND CONTINUITY

In every phase of our work . . . we constantly had occasion to speak of logic and continuity. . . . They are of prime importance. . . . Creating must be logical and have continuity. Even illogical and incoherent characters must be represented within the logical plan and framework of a whole play, a whole performance.

. . . How to accomplish this? By means of physical actions . . . because they are easier to establish, materially and visually, and are yet closely tied to all the other elements. . . . It is easier to orient one's self with their aid. . . . Having prepared a logical and coherent line of physical actions, . . . we discover that parallel to it will run a logical and coherent line of emotion. . . . Come to the tragic part of a role . . . gradually and logically, by carrying out correctly your sequence of external physical actions, and by believing in them. . . . Do not think about your emotions. Think about what you have to do. If you do not adhere strictly to an absolute pattern of logic and continuity you are in danger of conveying passions, images, actions in a "generalized" form.

If an actor keeps in constant exercise . . . he will come to know practically all human actions from the point of view of their component parts, their consecutiveness and their logic. But this work must be done daily, constantly, like the vocalizing of a singer, or the exercises of a dancer, . . . systematic and absolutely valid exercises of actions without props.

—*An Actor Prepares*
—*Building a Character*
—*My Life in Art*

See ACTION, PERFORMING "IN GENERAL," THROUGH LINE OF ACTION.

M

MAGIC IF

From the moment of the appearance of [the *Magic*] *If* the actor passes from the plane of actual reality into the plane of another life, created and imagined by him.

In order to be emotionally involved in the imaginary world which the actor builds on the basis of a play, in order to be caught up in the action on the stage, he must believe in it. . . . This does not mean he should give himself up to anything like hallucination, . . . quite the contrary. . . . He does not forget that he is surrounded by stage scenery and props. . . . He asks himself: "But if this were real, how would I react? What would I do?" . . . And normally, naturally . . . this *If* acts as a lever to lift him into a world . . . of creativity.

The secret of the effect of *If* [is] that it does not use fear or force. Another quality: it arouses an inner and real activity, . . . an instantaneous inner stimulus, . . . adds a whole series of contingencies based on your own experience in life, and you will see how easy it will be for you sincerely to believe in the possibility of what you are called upon to do on the stage.

—*An Actor Prepares*
—*My Life in Art*

See FAITH, IMAGINATION, SENSE OF TRUTH ON THE STAGE, SINCERITY OF EMOTIONS.

MAKE-UP

One feature in my make-up gave a living and comic expression to my face, and something suddenly turned within me. All that had been dim became clear, all that was groundless suddenly had ground under its feet, all that I did not believe in suddenly found my trust. . . . Something had ripened within me, slowly filling with life while it was in the bud, and now at last it bloomed. . . . An accidental touch of the make-up brush on my face served to open the flower of the role. . . .

Every actor should have an attitude of great respect, affection and attention for his make-up. It must not be laid on mechanically but, if one can say so, with psychology while he broods over the soul and life of his part. Then the slightest wrinkle will acquire its inner basis from something in life that produced it.

—*Collected Works, Vol. III*
—*My Life in Art*

See COSTUMES AND PROPERTIES.

MATERIAL FOR CREATIVENESS

You must constantly be adding to your store. For this purpose you draw . . . principally upon your own impressions, feelings and experiences. You also acquire material from life around you, real and imaginary, from reminiscences, books, art, science, knowledge of all kinds, from journeys, museums and above all from communication with other human beings.

We are asked to interpret the life of human souls all over the world. An actor creates not only the life of his times, but that of the past and future as well. That is why he needs to observe, conjecture, to experience, to be carried away with emotion. If his creation is to interpret the past, the future, or an imaginary epoch, he has either to reconstruct or to recreate something out of his imagination.

The inner experience of an actor, the circle of his living impressions and emotions, should certainly be constantly enlarged, because it is only under such conditions that an actor can extend the circle of his own creativeness.

—An Actor Prepares
—Collected Works, Vol. VI

See EMOTION MEMORY, IMAGINATION.

MEASURE—PROPORTION

We cannot leave things to chance; . . . an actor [must] know how to proceed under ordinary circumstances, when a whole act is too large to handle, how to break it up. If one detail is not sufficient, add others; . . . a sense of *measure* will help.

On the stage it is easy for an actor to lose his sense of measure. . . . It seems to him he is doing too little, that with a big audience he should do a lot more. . . . Knowing this peculiarity of the stage . . . [he] should not increase his activity, but rather cut three-fourths of it.

—An Actor Prepares
—Creating a Role

See CONTACT WITH THE AUDIENCE.

MECHANICAL ACTING

In mechanical acting there is no call [necessity] for a living process. . . . You will understand this better when you come to recognize the origins and methods of mechanical acting which we characterize as "rubber stamp." . . . Some of these established clichés have become traditional and are passed down from generation to generation . . . still others are invented by the actors themselves.

Time and constant habit make even . . . senseless things near and dear. . . . No matter how skilful an actor may be in his choice of stage conventions, because of their inherent mechanical quality, he cannot move the spectators by them, so he takes refuge in what we call theatrical emotions. They are a sort of artificial imitation of the periphery of physical feelings.

The very worst fact is that clichés will fill up every empty spot in a role, which is not already solid with living feeling. Moreover they often push in ahead of feeling, that is why an actor must protect himself most conscientiously against such devices. And this is true even of gifted actors, capable of true creativeness.

—An Actor Prepares

See CLICHÉ ACTING, THEATRICAL EMOTIONS.

MEMORY

At moments of intense creativeness one's memory may fail . . . and break the continuity of the line of transmitting the verbal text of the play. . . . This preoccupation with remembering the words, when an actor is unsure of himself . . . deprives him . . . of the capacity to give himself up freely and . . . wholly to his ardent creative mood. . . . It is all important for an actor to have a good memory.

—Collected Works, Vol. I

See LOGIC AND CONTINUITY.

METHOD
See WHAT IS MY SYSTEM?

MIRROR, USE OF
You must be very careful in the use of a mirror. It teaches an actor to watch the outside rather than the inside of his soul, both in himself and in his part.

—An Actor Prepares

MISE EN SCÈNE
The responsibility for creating this ensemble, for its artistic integrity, the expressiveness of the over-all performance lies with the director. In the period when the director was a despot . . . he worked out the whole plan of the production, he indicated the general outlines of the parts, taking into consideration, of course, the participating actors, and he showed them all the "business." . . . But now I have arrived at the conviction that the creative work of the director must proceed in unison with that of the actors and not outdistance it nor hold it back. He must facilitate the creativeness of the actors, supervise and integrate it, taking care that it evolves naturally and only from the true artistic kernel of the play. This joint work of the director and the actors, this search for the essential kernel of the plays, begins with analysis and proceeds along the line of *through-going action*. This applies also to the external shaping of a performance. That should be, in my opinion, the objective of a director nowadays.

—An Actor Prepares
—Stanislavski's Legacy

See DIRECTOR (RÉGISSEUR), DIRECTOR AS DICTATOR, THROUGH LINE OF ACTION.

MOB SCENES

See CROWD SCENES.

MOOD

See INNER CREATIVE STATE.

MUSCULAR TENSION

See RELAXATION OF MUSCLES

N

NAÏVETÉ

This is a precious asset for an actor. . . . It cannot be fabricated or the result is affectation. So be naïve to the extent that it is part of your nature to be so. Every actor is to some degree naïve. But in ordinary life he is embarrassed to show this quality so he masks it. Do not do that when you are on the stage. . . . In order to induce naïveté an actor should be concerned, not with the quality itself but with what promotes and also what interferes with it. The thing that interferes with it most of all is a spirit of carping criticism. In order to be naïve one cannot be over-meticulous and analytical when using one's imagination.

The greatest help to naïveté are faith and a sense of truth. . . . Therefore in the first instance seek out what is true for you and that in which you can have faith.

—*Collected Works, Vol. II*

See CARPING CRITICISM, FAITH, SENSE OF TRUTH ON THE STAGE.

NATURALISM

Those who think that we sought naturalism on the stage are mistaken. We never leaned toward such a principle. . . . We sought inner truth, the truth of feeling and experience.

Continuing to play the new for the sake of the new,

. . . we declared war on such an interpretation of peasant plays. We wanted to show the real muzhik [peasant] and not only the costume but also the inner physique of his soul. But . . . we had not reached the stage where we could interpret [the spiritual side]. In order to fill the void . . . we exaggerated the . . . external side. This remained without inner justification, for lifeless objects, properties, and sounds began to bulge out of the general scheme. This resulted in naked naturalism. And the nearer it was to reality . . . the worse it was. . . . Naturalism on the stage is only naturalism when it is justified by the inner experience of the actor. . . . I would advise all theoreticians who do not know this from their own experience to see my words tested on the stage.

You used naturalism for the sake of naturalism. . . . That kind of objective and that kind of scenic truth is anti-artistic.

—*An Actor Prepares*
—*My Life in Art*

See JUSTIFICATION, REALISM.

NATURE

The greatest artist we know [is] Nature, the creative nature of all artists, [which] is in all the centres and parts of our physical and spiritual make-up, even those of which we are not aware. We have no direct means of approaching her, but there exist oblique ones which are little known. . . . This admitted lack of knowledge . . . is the outgrowth of wisdom. . . . To me it is the urge to attain, with the help of a sensitive heart, the unattained. And it will be attained in time. In the expectation of these new triumphs of science I have felt there was nothing for me to do except to devote my labours and energy almost exclusively to the study of Creative Nature. . . . I have acquired a sum of experience in the course of long years of work and this is what I have sought to share with you.

The most powerful, vivid, and convincing adaptations are the products of that wonderworking artist—Nature. They are almost wholly of subconscious origin. . . . Here is an example of intuitive adjustment as an expression of supreme sorrow. In *My Life in Art* there is a description of how a mother received the news of the death of her son. In the first few moments she expressed nothing but began hurriedly to dress. Then she rushed to the street door and cried, "Help!"

An adjustment of that sort cannot be reproduced either intellectually or with the aid of technique. It is created naturally, spontaneously, unconsciously, at the very moment when emotions are at their height. Yet that type, so direct, vivid and convincing, represents the effective method we need. It is only by such means that we create and convey to an audience of thousands all the finer, barely perceptible shades of feeling. But to such experiences the only approach is through intuition and the subconscious.

In the realm of intuition and the subconscious I know nothing, except that these secrets are open to the great artist Nature.

You can go astray only if . . . you do not have confidence in Nature. . . . Nature's laws are binding on all, without exception, and woe to those who break them.

—*An Actor Prepares*
—*Building a Character*

See ADAPTATION, PSYCHO-TECHNIQUE, SUBCONSCIOUS.

O

OBJECTIVES

Life, people, circumstances . . . constantly put up barriers. . . . Each of these barriers presents us with the objective of getting through it. The division of a play into units, to study its structure, has one purpose. . . . There is another, far more important, inner reason. At the heart of every unit lies a *creative objective*. . . . Every objective must carry in itself the germs of action. . . . You should not try to express the meaning of your objective in terms of a noun . . . but . . . always employ a *verb*. . . . [e.g. "I wish" or "I wish to do—"] This objective engenders outbursts of desires for the purposes of creative aspiration. . . . It is important that an actor's objectives be in accordance with his capacities. . . . At first it is better to choose simple physical but attractive objectives. . . . Every physical objective will contain something of a psychological objective, they are indissolubly bound together. . . . Do not try too hard to define the dividing line, . . . go by your feelings always tipping the scales slightly in favour of the physical. . . . The right execution of a physical objective will help to create a right psychological state.

An actor should know how to distinguish among the qualities of objectives, avoiding the irrelevant ones and establishing those appropriate to his part. Appropriate objectives must be on our side of the footlights: personal yet analogous to those of the character portrayed; truthful so that you yourself, the actors playing with you and your audience, can believe in their clear-cut [purpose]. They must be distinctly woven into the fabric of your part; active . . . [to] push your role ahead and not let it stagnate. Let me warn you against . . . purely motor [objectives] which are prevalent in the theatre and lead to mechanical performance.

—An Actor Prepares
—Creating a Role

See COMMUNION, CREATIVE WILL, UNITS, SUPER-OBJECTIVE.

OBJECT OF ATTENTION

See ATTENTION.

OBSERVATION

An actor should be observant not only on the stage but also in real life. He should concentrate with all his being on whatever attracts his attention. . . . There are people gifted by nature with powers of observation. . . . When you hear such people talk you are struck by the amount that an unobservant person misses. . . . Average people have no conception of how to observe the facial expression, the look of the eye, the tone of the voice, in order to comprehend the state of mind of the persons with whom they talk. . . . If they could do this . . . their creative work would be immeasurably richer, finer and deeper. This . . . calls for a tremendous amount of work, time, desire to succeed, and systematic practice.

How can we teach unobservant people to notice what nature and life are trying to show them? First of all they must be taught to look at, listen to, and to hear what is beautiful. Such habits elevate their minds and arouse feelings which will leave deep traces in their emotion memories. Nothing in life is more beautiful than nature, and it should be the object of constant observation. . . . Take a little flower, or a petal from it, or a spider web, or a design made by frost on the window pane. Try to express in words what it is in these things that gives pleasure. Such an effort causes you to observe the object more closely, more effectively . . . and do not shun the darker side of nature. . . . Disfigurement often . . . sets off beauty. . . . Search out both beauty and its opposite, and define them, learn to know and see them. . . . Next turn to what the human race has produced in art, literature, music.

—*An Actor Prepares*

See ATTENTION, EMOTION MEMORY, MATERIAL FOR CREATIVENESS.

P

PAUSES IN SPEECH

The first work to be done with speech or with words is always to divide into measures, to place the . . . pauses. . . . The logical pause mechanically shapes the measures, whole phrases of the text, and thereby contributes to . . . intelligibility; the psychological pause adds life to the thoughts. . . . [It is an] eloquent silence.

It helps to convey the subtextual content of the words. If speech without the logical pause is unintelligible, without the psychological pause it is lifeless. . . . The logical pause serves our brain, the psychological our feelings. . . . There is one other kind of pause . . . just sufficient for a quick intake of breath. . . . The pause is an important element . . . in our technique of speech.

—Building a Character

See ACCENTUATION, INTONATIONS AND PUNCTUATION, SPEECH.

PERFORMANCE

It is only when it is performed on the stage that a play is revealed in all its fullness and essence. It is only then that the living soul of a play, of its text and subtext, is conveyed by the actors.

By adhering to their inner line of images the actors

remain true to the subtext and through line of action, and by the same token they renew their emotion memories which enable them to live their parts. . . . There may be certain variations but that is all to the good, as spontaneity and the unexpected are both excellent stimuli to creativity. . . . The tempo-rhythm of a play . . . is made up of a series of varying tempi and rhythms, harmoniously blended into a single whole. The overall effect may be one of grandeur, majesty, lightness, gaiety, according to whatever tempi and rhythm preponderate. Their importance in any given performance is in any case enormous. A fine play, well produced and acted, may not be successful because it is performed in too slow a tempo or hurried along at an inappropriately quick one. For actors, life on the stage represents real living. In every performance our life is to pursue a super-objective . . . along a through line of action among given circumstances.

When actors mature in their parts, and live in them, they can discard all superfluities. Then their roles are like crystals of emotions, harmonizing with the overall tone, rhythm, tempo of the production. Then the play is really ready to be performed before an audience.

> —*Building a Character*
> —*Collected Works, Vols. III and VI*
> —*Stanislavski's Legacy*

See ACTION, CREATIVE INTENT OF A PLAY, TEMPO-RHYTHM, THROUGH LINE OF ACTION, SPONTANEITY.

PERFORMING "IN GENERAL"

This phrase "in general" is the bane of the theatre. Its effect is to blur all emotional outlines and prevent an actor from feeling any solid ground on which he can stand with confidence. . . . In hurried or general descriptions we care very little whether what we transmit corresponds to reality. We are satisfied with any general characteristic or illusion.

These methods of portraying feeling "in general" exist in everyone of us. And they are used without any relation to the why, wherefore, or circumstances in which a person has experienced them. Such ham acting is elementary to a ridiculous degree.

On the stage there cannot be, under any circumstances, action which is directed immediately at the arousing of a feeling for its own sake. . . . Never seek to be jealous, or to make love, or to suffer, for its own sake. All such feelings are the result of something that has gone before.

True art and performing "in general" are incompatible. The one destroys the other. . . . Art does not tolerate "anyhow," "in general," "approximately."

—*An Actor Prepares*
—*Collected Works, Vol. II*
—*My Life in Art*

See CLARITY, LOGIC AND CONTINUITY.

PERSPECTIVE IN CHARACTER BUILDING

Perspective means: the calculated, harmonious inter-relationship and distribution of the parts in a whole play or role. . . . There can be no acting . . . without its appropriate perspective. Only after an actor has thought through, analyzed and felt himself to be a living person inside his whole part there opens up to him the long, beautiful beckoning perspective. . . .

Against this depth of background he can play out whole actions, speak whole thoughts. . . . When we come to the laying on of colour along the lines of artistic perspective, we again are obliged to adhere to qualities of consecutiveness, tone and harmony. As in painting, artistic colouring does a very great deal to make it possible to distinguish planes. . . . The important parts . . . are most highly coloured, whereas those relegated to the background are less vivid.

As a part moves along we have . . . two perspectives in mind. The one is related to the character portrayed, the other to the actor. Actually Hamlet, as a figure in a play . . . knows nothing of what the future has in store for him, whereas the actor who plays the part must bear this constantly in mind; he is obliged to keep in perspective.

We must not forget one extremely important quality inherent in perspective. It lends a breadth, a sweep, a momentum to our inner experiences and external actions.

Perspective and the through line of action are not identical but . . . the one is the other's closest aid.
                                        —*Building a Character*

See THROUGH LINE OF ACTION.

PHYSICAL ACTIONS

See ACTION.

PHYSICAL ATTENTION

See ATTENTION.

PLANES OF ACTING

See PERSPECTIVE IN CHARACTER BUILDING.

PLASTICITY OF MOTION

The more subtle the emotions, the greater the clarity, precision and plasticity needed to convey them in physical form. Among dramatic actors . . . some . . . use plasticity for the sole purpose of impressing their admirers of the opposite sex. . . . Other . . . actors have worked out for themselves a permanently fixed kind of plasticity and they pay no further attention to that side of their physical actions. . . . If they would lend an attentive ear to their own mechanics, they would sense an energy rising from the deepest wells of their being.... It is charged with emotions, desires, objectives . . . for the purpose of arousing this or that action. . . . Energy, heated by emotion, charged with will, directed by the intellect . . . manifests itself in . . . action, full of feeling, content and purpose . . . which cannot be carried out in any slipshod, mechanical way, but must be fulfilled in accordance with its spiritual impulses. Movement and action which . . . follow an inner pattern are essential to real artists in drama, ballet and other theatre and plastic arts. . . . This is also true of other arts. . . . Music must have that same unbroken line of sound and . . . can a painter achieve the simple outline of a drawing without it? . . . Art itself originates in the moment when that unbroken line is established, be it of sound . . . drawing or movement. . . . That is the motion which creates fluency, the plasticity of body movement which is so necessary.

At the foundation of plasticity of movement one must establish an inner flow of energy. . . . *External plasticity is based on our inner sense of the movement of energy.*

—*Building a Character*
—*Collected Works, Vol. II*

See BALLET, BODY TRAINING, EXTERNAL TECHNIQUE, TUMBLING.

PLAYWRIGHT DOMINATES

A theatre in which the most powerful personality is the playwright or . . . a literary director . . . becomes a *literary* theatre. . . . The principal place is occupied by . . . subtle interpretations of a playwright's work. In such theatres the interesting elements are: the general concepts of an approach to a play, the treatment of ideas, style, . . . characters, psychology, etc. . . . In every pose, intonation, gesture of an actor, . . . an idea is concealed, or some generalization, allegory, knowledge, etc.

The playwright's works are so successfully revealed by the literary director . . . that the other participants in the performance have . . . to submit to his creative initiative . . . and do all they can to convey . . . concisely, beautifully, the intent for the production of their talented literary director.

As a result you enjoy a large and honourable success, get serious reviews, stir arguments among the pundits, are the subject of essays. Yet has this theatre fulfilled its fundamental objective in art, has it created the life of a human spirit and clothed it in a beautiful physical form? No!

—*Stanislavski's Legacy*

See CREATIVE INTENT OF A PLAY, DIRECTOR AS DICTATOR, SCENE DESIGNER DOMINATES.

PLOT

There are plays (inferior comedies, melodramas, vaudeville, revues, farces) where the external plot is the mainspring of the action. The high points are the facts of a murder, a death, a wedding, the dumping of flour or water on one of the characters. . . . In other plays the plot as such has little significance. . . . In such plays it is not the facts but the relationship of the characters to them that constitutes the centre of interest. In such plays facts are needed only to the extent that they provide motivation and opportunity for the actors to express their inner content. Chekhov's plays are in this category. The best thing is when form and content are in complete harmony. There the life of a human spirit in a part is inseparable from the facts of the plot. . . . Let the actor learn by heart and write down the existing facts, their sequence and their external physical connection with one another. . . . With growing experience of the play and its contents this method helps not only to pick out the facts and orient oneself in relation to them but also to get at that inner substance, their interrelationships and interdependence.

—*Collected Works, Vol. IV*
—*Creating a Role*

See APPRAISING THE FACTS OF A PLAY, CREATIVE INTENT OF A PLAY, KERNEL OF A PLAY.

PRE-PERFORMANCE PREPARATION

Most actors before each performance put on costumes and make-up so that their external appearance will approximate that of the character they are to play. But they forget the most important part, which is the inner preparation. Why do they devote such particular attention to their external appearance? Why do they not put make-up and costume on their souls?

The inner preparation for a part is as follows: instead of rushing into his dressing-room at the last moment, an actor should (especially if he has a big part) arrive there two hours ahead of his entrance and begin to get himself in form. You know that a sculptor kneads his clay before he begins to use it, and a singer warms up his voice before a concert. We need to do something similar to tune our inner strings, to test the keys, the pedals, and the stops.

We must exercise great care, each time we have a creative piece of work to do, to prepare . . . a true inner creative mood. To prepare yourself, go over the fundamental parts of your role. You do not need to develop them fully. What you must do is ask: Am I sure of my attitude toward this or that particular place? Do I really feel this or that action? . . . Think up various suppositions and suggest possible circumstances into which you put yourself. . . . All these preparatory exercises test your expressive apparatus . . . and will tune up your inner creative instrument.

—*An Actor Prepares*

See INNER CREATIVE STATE ON THE STAGE.

PROPORTION, SENSE OF

See MEASURE.

PROPOSED CIRCUMSTANCES
See ACTION, GIVEN CIRCUMSTANCES.

PSYCHO-TECHNIQUE

In the soul of a human being there are certain elements . . . subject to consciousness and will. These accessible parts are capable in turn of acting on psychic processes. . . . To rouse your subconscious to creative work is a special technique.

In the first period of conscious work on a role, an actor feels his way into the life of his part, without altogether understanding what is going on in it, in him and around him. When he reaches the region of the subconscious the eyes of his soul are opened and he is aware of everything, even minute details, and it all acquires an entirely new significance. He is conscious of new feelings, conceptions, visions, attitudes, both in his role and in himself.

I do not give you any technical means to gain control of the subconscious. I can only teach you the indirect method to approach it and give yourselves up to its power.

When an actor is completely absorbed by some profoundly moving objective, so that he throws his whole being passionately into its execution, he reaches a state that we call inspiration. In it almost everything he does is subconscious and he has no conscious realization of how he accomplishes his purpose.

What happens of its own accord in real life, and in a natural manner, has to be prepared on the stage by the use of a psycho-technique.

—*An Actor Prepares*
—*Collected Works, Vol. II*

See ACTION, SUBCONSCIOUS, WHAT IS MY SYSTEM?

PUBLIC SOLITUDE

In a circle of light on the stage in the midst of darkness, you have the sensation of being entirely alone. . . . This is called solitude in public. . . . During a performance, before an audience of thousands, you can always enclose yourself in this circle, like a snail in its shell. . . . You can carry it with you wherever you go.

—An Actor Prepares

See ATTENTION.

R

REALISM

Among theatre leaders, actors, spectators, critics, there are many who prefer theatricality and artificiality. . . . They are surfeited with realistic actuality on the stage. . . . "Only not the way it is in real life!" they say. To get away from it they search out the most exaggerated anti-realistic forms.

In contrast to them are those . . . who prefer and accept in the theatre only natural truthfulness, realism. They are not afraid of the catharsis of their souls through powerful impressions. . . . All they want on the stage is a reflection of the real life of human souls.

In both cases there are excesses. . . . In the first the sharpness of the theatricality is carried to the point of the absurd and in the second the simplicity and "naturalness" is pushed to the limits of ultranaturalism. . . . For example: An actor exaggerates truth in a death scene to an undesirable degree . . . with cramps, nausea, groans, horrible grimaces . . . indulging in naturalism for its own sake . . . instead of being pre-occupied with the last moments of a human soul.

Truth on the stage . . . must be real, but rendered poetic through creative imagination. Impressionism, and other "isms" in art are accepted only in so far as they represent realism in a refined, enobled, distilled form.

—*An Actor Prepares*
—*Collected Works, Vols. II and VII*

See CONVENTION, NATURALISM, SENSE OF TRUTH ON THE STAGE.

RÉGISSEUR

See DIRECTOR.

REHEARSAL

An actor must constantly practice to achieve a true creative mood at all times, whether he is performing, rehearsing or working at home.

Some actors . . . have the insufferable habit of rehearsing . . . in barely perceptible, low tones when speaking their lines. . . . That can do nothing but form bad habits. . . . What is your partner to derive from such cues? . . . An actor is obligated to produce his part in full, to give the right responses to his partner, follow correctly the laid-out line of the play and respond to what is said to him by his partner. . . . Otherwise a rehearsal loses all meaning. If . . . everyone takes the right attitude towards collective obligations, comes to rehearsal properly prepared, then a splendid atmosphere is established.

There are many actors who . . . do not take creative initiative. . . . They come to the rehearsal and wait until they are led along a path of action. After great effort the régisseur can sometimes succeed in striking sparks in such passive natures. . . . Only we directors know how much work, inventiveness, patience, nervous strength and time it takes to push such actors of weak creative impulse ahead, away from their dead centre.

Need I explain that such drones who profit by the work and creativeness of others are an infinite drag on the accomplishment of the whole group. . . . One cannot rehearse at the expense of others. . . . Each actor must bring to rehearsal his own living emotions. . . . Actors are not puppets.

When you reach the stage of virtuosity in your psycho-technique . . . rehearsals go easily, quickly, and according to plan.

—*An Actor Prepares*
—*Building a Character*

See COLLECTIVE CREATIVENESS, HABIT, HOME-WORK, PRE-PERFORMANCE PREPARATION, PSYCHO-TECHNIQUE.

RELAXATION OF MUSCLES

You cannot . . . have any conception of the evil that results from muscular spasms and physical contraction. . . . Actors usually strain themselves in the exciting moments. Therefore at times of great stress it is especially necessary to achieve a complete freedom of muscles. In fact, in the high moments of a part the tendency to relax should become more normal than the tendency to contract. . . . Let the tenseness come . . . if you cannot avoid it. But immediately let your control step in and remove it. Until this control becomes a . . . habit . . . give a lot of thought to it. . . . Later, this relaxing of the muscles should become a normal phenomenon. . . . Among the nervous people of our generation this muscular tensity is inescapable. To destroy it completely is impossible, but we must struggle with it incessantly. . . . This . . . removal of unnecessary tenseness should be developed to the point where it becomes a normal habit and a natural necessity, not only during the quieter parts of your role, but especially at times of the greatest nervous and physical lift.

—*An Actor Prepares*

See ATTENTION, INNER TENSION, STAGE FRIGHT.

REPEATED FEELINGS

Do we, as a matter of fact, ever feel things [on the stage] for the first time? Feelings we have never experienced in real life? . . . These direct, powerful and vivid emotions do not make their appearance on the stage in the way you think. . . . They flash out in short episodes. . . . In that form they are highly welcome. . . . The unfortunate part about them is that we cannot control them. They control us. Therefore we have no choice but to leave it to nature. . . . We will only hope that they will work with the part and not at cross purposes to it.

An infusion of unexpected, unconscious feelings is very tempting. It is what we dream about, and it is a favourite aspect . . . of our art. But you must not . . . minimize the significance of *repeated feelings* drawn from emotion memory—on the contrary, you should be completely devoted to them, because they are the only means by which you can, to any degree, influence inspiration.

—*An Actor Prepares*

See EMOTION MEMORY, INSPIRATION, SPONTANEITY.

"REPRESENTATION" ACTING

In it the actor also lives his part. . . . This partial identity with our method . . . makes it possible to consider this other type also true art.

Yet the actor lives his part only as a preparation for perfecting an external form. . . . Once that is determined he reproduces that form through the aid of mechanically trained muscles. . . . Living your role is not the chief moment of creation . . . but one of the preparatory stages for further artistic work. . . . Often they [such actors] are extremely skilful in technique, and are able to get through a part with . . . no expenditure of nervous force; . . . they often think it unwise to feel.

This type of art is less profound than beautiful, it is more immediately effective than truly powerful; in it the form is more interesting than the content. . . . Delicate and deep human feelings are not subject to such technique. The art of representation demands perfection if it is to remain an art.

—An Actor Prepares

RESTRAINT IN GESTURES

An actor's performance which is cluttered up with a multiplicity of gestures will be like a messy sheet of paper. . . . Before he undertakes the external creation of his character . . . he must rid himself of all superfluous gestures. . . . [He] should so harness [them] that he will always be in control of them. . . . An excessive use of gesture dilutes a part. . . . In addition to gestures, actors . . . make many involuntary movements in an effort to help themselves over difficult spots in their parts. . . . Such movements take the form of compulsive cramps, needless as well as harmful overtenseness. . . . How agreeable it is to see an artist on the stage when he exercises restraint and does not indulge in all these convulsive, cramped gestures. We see the pattern of his part emerge distinctly because of that restraint . . .

Restraint of gesture is of particular importance in the field of characterisation. . . . It often happens that an actor can find only three or four characteristic typical gestures. To be satisfied throughout a whole play with that many gestures requires utmost economy of movement. . . . Characteristic gestures cannot . . . be repeated too often or they lose their effect.

Among the finest qualities of artists in the theatre who have achieved supreme rank are their restraint and finish.

—Building a Character

See EXTERNAL TECHNIQUE, GESTURE.

ROLE INSIDE THE ACTOR

Among the large number of parts played [by an actor] there are some that seem to have been creating themselves in his inner consciousness for a long time. He has only to touch it and it comes to life without any searching or mechanical preparation. . . . The role and its image have been created within him by nature itself. . . . The actor ceases to act, he begins to live the life of the play. . . . The author's words become his words. . . . This is a . . . *miracle* . . . for the sake of which we are willing to make any sacrifices, to be patient, suffer and work.

In . . . separate moments, or even throughout whole scenes, you feel yourself inside your role, in the atmosphere of the play, and some of the sensations of the character you portray come very close to your own. . . . This merging with your part we call the achievement of a sense of being inside your part, and its being inside of you.

It is a great piece of good fortune when an actor can instantly grasp the play with his whole being, his mind and his feelings. In such happy but rare circumstances it is better to forget all about laws and methods, and give himself up to the power of creative nature. But these circumstances are so rare that one cannot count on them. They are as rare as the moments when an actor immediately grasps an important line of direction, a basic section of a play. . . . Why is it that some parts of a play come to life . . . while others [leave us] without feeling? . . . That happens because the places which are infused with immediate life are congenial to us, familiar to our emotions. . . . Later on, when we become better acquainted with and feel closer to the play, . . . we shall find that [these] . . . points of light grow . . . until they finally fill out our entire role.

—*Creating a Role*

See HERE AND NOW, FIRST ACQUAINTANCE WITH A PLAY.

RUBBER STAMP

See CLICHÉ ACTING, MECHANICAL ACTING.

S

SALVINI, TOMMASO

See DOUBLE FUNCTION, LIVING A PART, VOICE.

SCENE DESIGNER DOMINATES

Let us suppose that the scene designer is paramount [in a theatre]. It is only natural that his talent will put the painting of the sets to the fore. Then the underlying . . . essence of the play will be sensed more vividly in colours, in the sets, in the painting-like compositions of group scenes. . . . The stage . . . will be . . . an exhibition of the product of a painter. In this visual holiday the actor is scarcely more than a clothes horse for the artistic costumes of the painter . . . [who] stylizes man according to the whim of his own fantasy, in lines that cannot be conveyed in action.

In recent years more and more theatres have been founded on the tyranny of the scene designer.

There have been genuinely artistic productions, startling indeed in their external beauty and variety. . . . The work of a scene designer in such a theatre is self-sufficient, it excites the public. . . . The public, the director of the play and the actors themselves fall prey to the enchantment and talent of the scene designer.

—*Stanislavski's Legacy*

See DIRECTOR AS DICTATOR, PLAYWRIGHT DOMINATES.

SCENERY AND PROPERTIES

Scenery and properties, all the externals of a production, are of value only in so far as they enhance the expressiveness of the dramatic action, the *acting*. . . . Light and sound play an important part in our inner lives: twilight, a mist, or a sunset have an entirely different effect on us from a sunrise. . . . But [on the stage] they are effective only when they are permeated by artistic truth, and are not just everyday, humdrum facts. . . . In other words it is of no matter whether the scenery is conventional, stylized or realistic, . . . we can welcome any setting provided only that it is appropriate. Life is itself so complex and varied that there are not enough kinds of scenic inventiveness to do full justice to all its aspects. . . . The important thing is that the sets and the whole production of a play be convincing . . . to the audience and to the actors.

—Collected Works, Vol. VI

See COSTUMES AND ACCESSORIES, EMOTION MEMORY, SCENE DESIGNER DOMINATES, STAGE SETTINGS, STIMULI TO EMOTION MEMORY.

SCORE OF A ROLE

Let us call this long catalogue of minor and major objectives, units, scenes, acts, the *score of a role*. . . . One can call them natural objectives. There can be no doubt that such a score, based on such objectives, will draw the actor—physically speaking—closer to the real life of his part. [It] . . . stirs the actor to physical action.

The first requirement is that the score have the

power to attract, . . . excite the actor not only by its
external physical truth but above all by its inner
beauty. . . . Let us now add depth to the score. . . .
The difference will lie in the inner life . . . inner impulses, psychological intimations . . . that constitute
the *inner tone*. . . . We can experience varying emotions when playing a score with the same objectives
but in different keys . . . quiet or joyful . . . sad or
. . . disturbed or in an excited key. . . . One's score
which is to portray human passions, must be rich,
colourful, and varied. . . . An actor must know the
nature of a passion . . . how to cull [from the text]
the component units, objectives, moments, which in
their sum total add up to a human passion. . . . The
score saturates every particle of an actor's inner being.
. . . In this innermost . . . core . . . all the remaining objectives converge, as it were, into one super-
objective . . . the concentration of the entire score.
. . . For the actor the through action is the *active
attainment of the super-objective*.

—*Creating a Role*

See STIMULI TO EMOTION MEMORY, SUPER-OBJECTIVE.

SELF-CRITICISM

Fear your admirers! Learn in time to hear, understand and love the cruel truth about yourselves. . . .
Talk of your art only with those who can tell you the
truth.

The majority of actors are afraid of the truth not
because they cannot bear it, but because it can break
in the actor his faith in himself.

—*My Life In Art*

See CARPING CRITICISM, EXHIBITIONISM.

SENSE OF TRUTH ON THE STAGE

A sense of truth is the best stimulus to emotion, imagination, creativeness. . . .

At the base of every art is a reaching out for artistic truth. The actor must believe in everything that takes place on the stage and most of all . . . in what he himself is doing and one can believe only in the truth. . . .

There is no such thing as actuality on the stage. Art is the product of the imagination, as the work of a dramatist should be. The aim of the actor should be to turn the play into a theatrical reality. . . . Everything must be real in the imaginary life of an actor.

Scenic truth is not like truth in life; it is peculiar to itself. . . . We are not concerned with the actual naturalistic existence of what surrounds us on the stage, the reality of the material world. This is of use to us only in so far as it supplies a general background for our feelings. . . . What counts . . . is not the material out of which Othello's dagger is made, be it steel or cardboard, but the inner feeling of the actor who can justify his suicide . . . [as] if the circumstances and conditions . . . were real. . . . It is necessary for the actor to develop to the highest degree his imagination, a childlike naïveté, . . . an artistic sensitivity to truth . . . in his soul, and body.

—*An Actor Prepares*
—*My Life in Art*

See ARTISTIC TRUTH—NATURAL BEAUTY, FAITH, IMAGINARY OBJECTS, NAÏVETÉ, SINCERITY OF EMOTIONS.

SENSORY ATTENTION

See ATTENTION.

SINCERITY OF EMOTIONS

Pushkin spoke of "sincerity of emotions, feelings that seem true in given circumstances." . . . That is exactly what we ask of an actor. We filter through ourselves all the materials that we receive from the author and the director; we work over them supplementing them out of our own imagination. That material becomes part of us, spiritually, even physically; our emotions are sincere. . . . Once you have established . . . contact between your life and your part . . . you will see how easy it will be for you sincerely to believe in the possibility of what you are called upon to do on the stage.

—An Actor Prepares

See APHORISM OF PUSHKIN.

SOLILOQUY

When do we talk to ourselves? Whenever we are so stirred up that we cannot contain ourselves; or when wrestling with some idea difficult to assimilate, when we are making an effort to memorize something and trying to impress it on our consciousness by saying it aloud, or when we relieve our feelings . . . by voicing them. These occasions are rare in ordinary life yet frequent on the stage. When I have occasion to commune with my own feelings on the stage, in silence, I enjoy it. . . . But when I am obliged to pronounce long . . . soliloquies I have no notion what to do. How can I find a basis for doing on the stage what I do not do off it? In addition to our brain . . . as the nerve and psychic centre of our being, we have a similar source near the heart. . . . I tried to establish communication between these two centres. . . . The sensation was that my brain held intercourse with my feelings. . . . I was able to commune with myself, either audibly or in silence, and with perfect self-possession.

—*An Actor Prepares*

See COMMUNION.

SPEECH

We need firm foundations for our art . . . in particular the art of speech and the ability to speak verse.

Musical speech opens up endless possibilities of conveying the inner life [we experience] on the stage. . . . What can we express with . . . our ordinary register of five or six notes? . . . We realize how ridiculous we are . . . [when] we have to convey complicated emotions. It is like playing Beethoven on a balalaika. . . . Speech is music. Pronunciation on the stage is as difficult an art as singing. It requires training and a technique bordering on virtuosity. . . . When an actor adds the vivid ornament of sound to the living content of the words, he causes me to glimpse with an inner vision the images he has fashioned out of his own creative imagination. . . . Every actor must be in possession of excellent diction and pronunciation. . . . He must feel not only phrases and words, but also each syllable, each letter.

You cannot bring back the spoken word. . . . Poor speech . . . even conceals the thought, . . . its very plot. . . . The audience will . . . begin to fidget . . . and finally to cough. . . . This spells ruin for the play. . . . One means of guarding against this is the use of clear, beautiful, vivid speech. To an actor a word is not just a sound, it is the evocation of images. . . .

Your job is to instill your inner visions in others . . .
and convey it in words.

—Building a Character

See INTONATIONS AND PUNCTUATION, PAUSES IN SPEECH,
SPEECH TEMPO-RHYTHM.

SPEECH TEMPO-RHYTHM

Letters, syllables, words—these are the musical notes
of speech, out of which to fashion measures, arias,
whole symphonies. There is good reason to describe
beautiful speech as musical.

Words spoken with resonance and sweep are more
affecting. In speech as in music there is a great difference between a phrase enunciated in whole, quarter
or sixteenth notes, or with triplets or quintuplets
thrown in. . . . In the first instance there is calm, in
the second nervousness, agitation.

Many actors who are careless of speech, inattentive
to words, pronounce them with such thoughtless slipshod speed, without putting any endings on them,
that they end up with completely mutilated, half
spoken phrases.

In proper and beautiful speech there should not be
any of these manifestations, except where a change of
tempo-rhythm is called for on purpose for the characterisation of a part.

Our difficulty lies in the fact that many actors lack
a well-rounded training in two important elements
of speech; on the one side there is smoothness, resonance, fluency, and on the other, rapidity, lightness,
clarity, crispness in the pronounciation of words.

To achieve stately, slow speech we need first of all to

replace silent pauses with sonorous cadences, the sustained singing tone of the words.

It will help you to read aloud very slowly to the timing of a metronome, if you are careful to preserve the smooth flow of words in rhythmic measures and also if you provide yourselves with the right inner basis for your exercise.

A clear-cut rhythm of speech facilitates rhythmic sensibility and the opposite is also true: the rhythm of sensations experienced helps to produce clear speech. Of course, all this occurs in the cases where the precision of speech is thoroughly based on inner, suggested circumstances and the "magic if."

Poetry arouses different emotions because of its different form from prose. But the converse is also true. Poetry has another form because we sense its subtext in a different way.

One of the main differences between spoken prose and verse forms lies in their having different tempo-rhythms, in the fact that their measures differ in their influence on our sensations, memories, our emotions. . . . Even if we do not understand the meaning of words their sounds affect us through their tempo-rhythms. . . . Think . . . of verses in which tempo-rhythm paints sound pictures, such as the ringing of bells or the clatter of horses' hooves.

There is an indissoluble interdependence, interaction and bond between tempo-rhythm and feeling and, conversely, between feeling and tempo-rhythm. . . . The correctly established tempo-rhythm of a play or a role, can of itself, intuitively (on occasion automatically) take hold of the feelings of an actor and arouse in him a true sense of living his part.

The direct effect on our mind is achieved by the words, the text, the thought, which arouse consideration. Our will is directly affected by the super-objective, by other objectives, by a through line of action. Our feelings are directly worked upon by tempo-rhythm.

Where does this lead us? . . . To the inescapable conclusion offered us by the wide possibility inherent in our psycho-technique, namely that we possess a direct, immediate means to stimulate every one of our inner motive forces.

—*Building a Character*

See INNER MOTIVE FORCES, PSYCHO-TECHNIQUE, SPEECH, THROUGH LINE OF ACTION.

SPIRITUAL REALISM

See LIVING A PART.

SPOKEN LINES

Words and the way they are spoken show up much more on the stage than in ordinary life. . . . An actor should know his own tongue in every particular. Of what use will all the subtleties of emotion be if they are expressed in poor speech?

Lines, repeated so often in rehearsals and numerous performances, are parroted. The inner content of the text evaporates, all that is left is mechanical sound.

Save your lines for two important reasons: so they will not be worn threadbare, and so that no mechanical chattering will disturb the basic pattern of the subtext.

—*Building a Character*

See SPEECH, SPEECH TEMPO-RHYTHM.

SPONTANEITY

A constant supply of spontaneity—is the only way to keep a role fresh, on the move. Lacking this it is likely to fade after a few performances. . . . The *unexpected* is often a most effective lever in creative work.

—*An Actor Prepares*
—*Collected Articles, Speeches, Talks, Letters*

See IMPROVISATION, NATURE, TRICKS-EFFECTIVE ADAPTATIONS.

STAGE FRIGHT

The most important [difficulty] is the abnormal circumstance of an actor's creative work—it must be done in public . . . [and] muscular tautness [which] interferes with inner emotional experience . . . will set in whenever [an actor] appears in public. . . . I remembered helping a man pick up nails that had fallen on the stage, when I was rehearsing. . . . Then I was absorbed by the simple act . . . and I forgot the black hole beyond the footlights. . . . I realized that from the very moment I concentrated on something behind the footlights I ceased to think about what was going on in front of them.

In ordinary life you walk and sit and talk and look but on the stage you lose these faculties. You feel the closeness of the public and you say to yourself, "Why are they looking at me?" . . . All our acts become strained . . . before a public of a thousand people.

When I stepped away from the darkness of the wings to the full illumination of the footlights, borderlights and spotlights, I felt blinded . . . but soon my eyes became accustomed to the light . . . and the fear and the attraction of the public seemed stronger than ever.

I was ready to turn myself inside out, . . . yet inside of me I had never felt myself so empty. The effort to squeeze out more emotion than I had, the powerlessness to do the impossible, filled me with a fear that turned my face and hands to stone. All my forces were spent on unnatural and fruitless efforts. . . . I was making a failure, and in my helplessness I was suddenly seized with rage. For several minutes I cut loose from everything about me. I flung out the famous line "Blood, Iago, Blood!" I felt in these words all the injury to the soul of a trusting man. . . . It almost seemed for a moment the listeners strained forward, and that through the audience there ran a murmur. The moment I felt this approval a sort of energy boiled up in me. I cannot remember how I finished the scene, because the footlights and the black hole disappeared from my consciousness, and I was free of all fear.

—*An Actor Prepares*

See ATTENTION, INNER CREATIVE STATE, PUBLIC SOLITUDE, RELAXATION OF MUSCLES.

STAGE SETTINGS

Surroundings have a great influence over your feelings. . . . When the external production of a play is inwardly tied up with the spiritual life of the actors it often acquires more significance on the stage than in real life. If it . . . produces the right mood it helps the actor to formulate the inner aspect of his role, it influences his whole psychic state and capacity to feel. Under such conditions the setting is a definite stimulus to our emotions.

—*An Actor Prepares*

See SCENERY AND PROPERTIES, STIMULI TO EMOTION MEMORY.

STIMULI TO EMOTION MEMORY

The usual impression is that a director uses all his material means, such as the set, the lighting, sound effects, and other accessories, for the primary purpose of impressing the public. On the contrary. We use these means more for their effect on the actors, . . . [as] external stimuli . . . calculated to create an illusion of real life and its living moods. . . . Another important source of stimulation of emotion is true physical action and your *belief* in it. . . . You will become acquainted with many new inner sources of stimulation. The most powerful of them lies in the text of the play, the implications of thought that underlie it and affect the interrelationship of the actors. . . . All these represent your psycho-technical store of riches, which you must learn to use. . . . If your [artistic emotions] do not come to the surface spontaneously, . . . concentrate your attention on the most effective kind of lure for them. . . . The bond between the lure and the feeling is natural and normal and one that should be extensively employed.

—An Actor Prepares

See COSTUMES AND ACCESSORIES, EMOTION MEMORY, SCENERY AND PROPERTIES, STAGE SETTING.

SUBCONSCIOUS

One of the main objectives pursued in our approach to acting is [the] natural stimulus to the creativeness of organic nature and its subconsciousness. . . . Our technique [is] directed . . . towards putting our subconscious to work (in the creation of artistic truth) and . . . to learning how not to interfere with it once it is in action.

It is fair to say that this technique bears the same relation to subconscious creative nature as grammar does to poetry. . . . We see, hear, understand, and think differently *before* and *after* we cross the threshold of the subconscious. . . . Our freedom on *this* side . . . is limited by reason and conventions; *beyond* it, our freedom is bold, wilful, active, and always moving forward. . . . Sometimes the tide of the subconscious barely touches an actor and then goes out. At other times it envelops his whole being, carrying him into its depth until, at length, it casts him up again on the shore of consciousness.

It is all very pleasant to think that every bit of creativeness is full of . . . exaltation and complexities. As a matter of actual fact, we find that even the smallest action of sensation, the slightest technical means, can acquire a deep significance on the stage. . . . When this point is reached, your whole spiritual and physical make-up will function normally, just as it does in real life. . . . I want you to feel right from the start, if only for short periods, that blissful sensation which actors have when their creative faculties are functioning truly, and unconsciously. Moreover, this is something you must learn through your own emotions and not in any theoretical way. You will learn to love this state and constantly strive to achieve it.

—*An Actor Prepares*
—*Building a Character*

See INNER CREATIVE STATE, LIVING A PART, PSYCHO-TECHNIQUE.

SUBTEXT

At the moment of performance the text is supplied by the playwright, and the subtext by the actor. . . . If this were not the case, people would not go to the theatre but sit at home and read the play. We are . . . inclined to forget that the printed play is not a finished piece of work until it is played on the stage by actors and brought to life by genuine human emotions; the same can be said of a musical score, it is not really a symphony until it is executed by an orchestra of musicians in a concert. As soon as people, either actors or musicians, breathe life of their own into the subtext of a piece of writing to be conveyed to an audience, the spiritual wellsprings, the inner essence are released. . . . The whole point of any such creation is the underlying subtext.

The line of a role is taken from the subtext, not from the text itself. But actors are lazy about digging down to the subtext; they prefer to skim along the surface, using the fixed words which they can pronounce mechanically, without wasting any energy in searching out their inner essence. . . . As this is, unfortunately, elusive and difficult to pin down, especially under the exciting and distracting circumstances of public performance, . . . we have to have recourse to inner vision, thought, inner action.

Words to an actor are not mere sounds, they are designs of visual images. . . . The best way to avoid mechanical acting, the mechanical rattling off of the text of a role . . . is to communicate to others what you see on the screen of your inner vision. . . . This will not be a reflection of reality but images created by your imagination to suit the needs of the imaginary character you are playing. It is up to you to convert these images into reality. . . . Each time you repeat the creative process of speaking the lines of your part, review in advance the series of prepared images on the screen of your inner vision.

The most substantial part of a subtext lies in its thought . . . that conveys the line of logic and coherence in a most clear-cut, definite way. . . . One thought gives rise to a second, a third, and all together shape a super-objective. . . . At times the intellectual content of the subtext may predominate, . . . at others the lines of inner vision. It is best when they merge. . . . Then the spoken word is filled with action. Words are . . . part of the external embodiment of an inner essence of a role. . . . When you reach the point when words are necessary to you to execute your objective, to your best purpose . . . you will reach for the author's text as joyfully as a violinist reaches for the Amati instrument offered to him; he knows that it will be the best means to express the feelings he harbours inside the depths of his soul.

> —*Building a Character*
> —*Collected Works, Vol. III*
> —*Creating a Role*

See ELEMENTS OF THE INNER CREATIVE STATE, INNER VISION, PSYCHO-TECHNIQUE, SUPER-OBJECTIVE, TEXT.

SUPER-OBJECTIVE

We use the word super-objective to characterize the essential idea, the core, which provided the impetus for the writing of a play. . . . In a play the whole stream of individual minor objectives, all the imaginative thoughts, feelings and actions of an actor should converge to carry out this super-objective. . . . Also this impetus toward the super-objective must be continuous throughout the whole play.

You cannot reach the super-objective by means of your . . . mind. The super-objective requires complete surrender, passionate desire, unequivocal action.

The most powerful stimuli to subconscious creativeness . . . are the through line of action and the super-objective . . . they are the principal factors in art.

—An Actor Prepares
—Creating a Role

See KERNEL OF A PLAY OR PART, OBJECTIVES, THROUGH LINE OF ACTION.

SYMBOLISM

It is a hard nut to crack—the symbol. It is successful when it has its source not in the mind, but in the inner soul. In this sense symbol and grotesque are alike. It is necessary to play a role hundreds of times, to crystallize its essence, to perfect the crystal, and in showing it, to interpret the quintessence of its contents. The symbol and the grotesque synthesize feelings and life. They gather in bright, daring and compressed form the multiform contents of the role.

Symbolism, impressionism and other highly distilled "isms" belong in the realm of the superconscious and begin where ultra-naturalism leaves off. But it is only when the inner and outer life of an actor on the stage is developed naturally . . . in accordance with the laws of nature that the superconscious will emerge from its secret sources.

—Collected Works, Vol. 1
—My Life in Art

See GROTESQUE, NATURALISM, REALISM.

T

TALENT

Talent is not easy to define or dissect. . . . Talent is often buried deep . . . and difficult to evoke.

Talent is the felicitous combination of many creative capacities in a person, governed by his generative will.

Technique exists above all for those who possess talent [and] inspiration. . . . It serves consciously to stimulate superconscious creativity. The more talent the actor has the more he cares about his technique.

A true creative state while on the stage, and all the elements that go to compose it, were the natural endowment of Shchepkin, Ermolova, Duse, Salvini. Nevertheless, they worked unremittingly on their technique. . . . Inspiration came to them by natural means almost every time they repeated a role, yet all their lives they sought an approach to it.

In our art it is very dangerous to mature too rapidly . . . without determined effort. . . . A talent may be no more than a pretty toy rattle. Talent includes physical attributes . . . memory, imagination, sensitiveness, impressionability. . . . A person may be ugly in real life . . . but fascinating on the stage, and that is better than being beautiful. One may have only a modicum of various qualities but make a powerful effect if possessed of stage charm. On the contrary a much larger talent may be utterly ineffective, lacking the power to attract.

—*Building a Character*
—*Collected Works, Vol. V*

See CHARM, DISCIPLINE, GENIUS, INSPIRATION, PSYCHO-TECHNIQUE.

TECHNIQUE

See PSYCHO-TECHNIQUE, TALENT, WHAT IS MY SYSTEM?

TEMPO-RHYTHM IN MOVEMENT

It is . . . more demonstrable to speak of inner tempo-rhythm at the same time as outer tempo-rhythm —when it becomes manifest in physical actions.

In collective action and speech on the stage you will have to find out and extract from the general chaos of tempo-rhythms those you need and then regroup them so that you can shape your own independent, individual lines of speed or measures of speech, movements, emotional experience in the roles being played by you. . . . The right measure of syllables, words, speech, movements in actions, together with their clear-cut rhythm is of profound significance to an actor. . . . Tempo-rhythm does possess the magic power to affect your inner mood. . . . [It] excites not only your emotion memory, . . . but it also brings your visual memory and its images to life. That is why it is wrong to take tempo-rhythm to mean only measure and speed.

We need it in combination with given circumstances which create a mood, we need it for the sake of its own inner substance. A military march, a stroll, a funeral procession may all be measured in the same tempo-rhythm, yet what a world of difference between them as to their inner content . . . which nourishes our feelings.

We . . . think, dream, grieve about things to ourselves in a special tempo-rhythm because each moment is manifest in our lives. Wherever there is life there is action; wherever action, movement; where movement,

tempo; and where there is tempo there is rhythm. . . .
If an actor is intuitively right in sensing what is being
said and done on the stage the correct tempo-rhythm
will be created of its own accord. . . . We deal with
tempo-rhythm the same way a painter does with
colours; we make combinations of all sorts of different speeds and measures. . . . Different rhythms and
tempi are to be found in simultaneous action not only
among the various actors performing in the same scene
at the same time, but also inside one of them. At the
point when the hero of the play or some particular
person has to take a definite and strong stand there
are no contradictions and doubts—one all-embracing
tempo-rhythm is not only appropriate, it is even necessary.

But when, as in Hamlet's soul, resolution wrestles
with doubt, various rhythms in simultaneous conjunction are necessary. In such cases several different tempo-
rhythms provoke an internal struggle of contradictory
origins. This heightens the actor's experience of his
part, reinforces inner activity and excites feelings.

The tempo-rhythm of a whole play is the tempo-
rhythm of the through line of action and the subtextual
content of the play.

—Building a Character

See ACTION, EMOTION MEMORY.

TERMINOLOGY

You cannot talk to actors in dry scientific language
and indeed . . . I could not do it in any case. My
task is to talk to an actor in his own language, not in
order to philosophize about art . . . but rather to
. . . define creative feelings in verbal terms.

Unfortunately . . . some of my fellow actors and followers adopted my terminology without testing its meanings; they understood me with their heads but not their feelings. What is even worse is that they were completely satisfied with this, . . . they spread my terminology, and purported to teach my method. . . . Nothing can be more harmful to art than the use of a method for its own sake. . . . The means may not be converted into the end goal.

—*Collected Works, Vols. I and II*
—*Stanislavski's Legacy*

See WHAT IS MY SYSTEM?

TEXT

To become the partner of the playwright, to perform his work on the stage, the actor must not only absorb the theme as a whole, but also its verbal form. He must not only know the words but take them into himself organically until he has transformed . . . them into his very own.

[Words] not impregnated with inner feeling, or [spoken] separately without relationship [to others] are so many empty sounds. . . . Yet the simplest words, if they convey complex thoughts can change our whole outlook on life. . . . Words can arouse all our five senses. . . . Words on the stage must never lack feeling . . . ideas . . . action. . . . The creative value of the text of a play is in its inner content, in its *subtext*.

—*Building a Character*
—*Creating a Role*

See SUBTEXT.

THEATRE

One of a human being's principal feelings is a
. . . longing for beauty . . . life-giving beauty. . . .
Science, knowledge, bereft of aesthetic quality, is arid,
. . . for that quality is what ennobles and enlivens
everything it touches.

The field of aesthetics is the field of the theatre. The
theatre possesses the greatest riches, the most powerful
means for affecting thousands of spectators at one time
and arousing their artistic emotions. The art of the
theatre is so vivid, pictorial, it illustrates a play so
fully . . . that it is accessible to all from professor to
peasant, from youth to old age.

Good theatre will always exist and be the prime goal
of the art of the actor.

—*Collected Works, Vol. VI*

See ARTISTIC TRUTH—NATURAL BEAUTY.

THEATRE STUDIO

This is neither a ready-made theatre nor a school for
beginners, but a laboratory for more or less mature
actors.

A Studio should offer an opportunity to its members
for testing their creative powers. It should facilitate the
exploratory work of scene designers, directors of plays
and all the others who work in the theatre. . . . Before an artist goes to work on a big painting he makes
many sketches. If he is not satisfied with one of them
he tears it up and makes another. . . . But in the
theatre one cannot tear up the scenery, the many
costumes, the necessary adjuncts of any enterprise on
the stage. And what about the tremendous human
forces expended on it?

Our art is collective and complex. Even its trial sketches are costly in money and effort. But a Studio, thanks to its modest dimensions, although it does not obviate the difficulties and expenses of trial sketches, nevertheless does offer the possibility of making them.

In every theatre there are capable artists who for one reason or another are not thoroughly caught up in their work. . . . Let them and directors of plays go into Studios and put on a series of productions. . . . In order to develop artistic creativeness they must have initiative and that is possible to develop only when there is a free field in which to do so. . . . Each will arrive at the goal of our art in his own way, through his own mistakes and his own achievements.

Look to the oldsters in the theatre for experience, wisdom, endurance, and to the youngsters for *effective initiative and intense devotion to work.*

　　　　　　　　　　—Collected Works, Vol. VI
　　　　　　　　　　—My Life in Art

THEATRICAL EMOTIONS

I took simple theatrical emotions—a kind of hysterical fit—as an outburst of inspiration . . . and I was mistaken.

No matter how skilful an actor may be in his choice of stage conventions, because of their inherent mechanical quality he cannot move the spectators by them. He must have some supplementary means of arousing them, so he takes refuge in what we call theatrical emotions. These are a sort of artificial imitation of the periphery of physical feelings.

If you clench your fists and stiffen the muscles of your body, or breathe spasmodically, you can bring yourself to a state of great physical intensity. This is often thought by the public to be an expression of a powerful temperament aroused by passion.

Actors of a more nervous type can arouse theatrical emotions by artificially screwing up their nerves; this produces theatrical hysteria, an unhealthy ecstasy which is usually just as lacking in inner content as is the artificial physical excitement.

In either case we are not dealing with acting art, but with false acting. Here are no true feelings of the actor as a human being as adapted to the role he is playing —what we have is theatrical emotion. Nevertheless this kind of emotion does have its effect, it hints at life, makes something of an impression; because many people are not capable of discriminating in the quality of the impression made, they are satisfied with a coarse imitation of emotions. Even the actors of this type are themselves often convinced that they are serving the ends of true art.

Muscular stimulation which derives not from feelings but from sheer mechanical strain, excludes all possibility of thought and true emotional experience.

—An Actor Prepares
—My Life in Art

See CLICHÉ ACTING, MECHANICAL ACTING.

THROUGH LINE OF ACTION

The main theme . . . gave birth to the writing of the play. It should also be the fountainhead of the actor's artistic creation.

That inner line of effort that guides the actors from the beginning to the end of the play we call *continuity* or the *through-going action.* . . . The main line of action and the main theme are organically part of the play and they cannot be disregarded without detriment to the play itself. The through line of action is a most powerful stimulant . . . and means of affecting the subconscious.

That inner line . . . galvanizes all the small units and objectives . . . and directs them toward the super-objective. From then on they all serve the common purpose. . . . Also this impetus . . . must be continuous.

—*An Actor Prepares*

See EMOTION AND LOGIC, LOGIC AND CONTINUITY, SUBCONSCIOUS, SUPER-OBJECTIVE.

TRADITIONS

The art [of the theatre] is created . . . by geniuses and talent. . . . What they do dies with them, but their legacy of creativeness, traditions, credos by which they were unconsciously guided at the beginning of their artistic careers and which they became aware of and formulated in their more mature years, remain for posterity. . . . Yet it is difficult to ascertain the spiritual essence of these traditions, put into words, or to catch their aroma . . . often the whole accomplishment of a lifetime is summed up in a brief formula. Such a distillation of a whole life of artistic activity can be an endless source [of interpretations] . . . and we must broaden, deepen, heighten the meaning of mere words.

The greatest tradition of this kind is to be found, according to my way of thinking, in the sayings of M. S. Shchepkin and Gogol.

An artistic creation on the stage lives for a moment, yet no matter how magnificent it may be, it cannot be retained. . . . The tradition of acting art lives on only in the talents and the capacities of actors.

In all ages it has been only the talented actors who have understood which traditions were worthy of survival.

By contrast, false traditions of performances, which once were infused with the feelings of great actors . . . have been handed down to us from generation to generation in an infinite number of artificial ways of external acting, manner of declaiming, external expressions of all sorts of emotions. . . . They can be only negative in meaning for us.

—Collected Works, Vol. V

See CLICHÉ ACTING, MECHANICAL ACTING, TALENT, TRUE ACTING.

TRAGEDY

If you tell an actor that his role is full of psychological actions, tragic depths, he will immediately begin to contort himself, exaggerate his passion, "tear it to tatters." . . . But if you give him some simple physical problem to solve . . . he will set about carrying it out without alarming himself or even thinking too deeply whether what he is doing will result in psychology, tragedy or drama.

To reach the great tragic heights an actor must stretch his creative power to the utmost. That is difficult in the extreme. . . . This state is brought about only by creative fervour, and that you cannot easily force. If you use unnatural means you are apt to go off in some false direction. . . . To avoid that error you must have hold of something substantial, tangible. The significance of physical acts in highly tragic or dramatic moments is emphasized by the fact that the simpler they are, the easier it is to grasp them.

The approach to drama and tragedy, or to comedy and vaudeville, differs only in the given circumstances which surround the *actions* of the person you are portraying. In the circumstances lie the main power and meaning of these actions. Consequently, when you are called upon to experience tragedy do not think about your emotions at all. Think about what you have to *do*.

A person in the midst of experiencing a poignant emotional drama is incapable of speaking of it coherently, for at such times tears choke him, his voice breaks. . . . But time, the great healer, . . . makes it possible for him to bear himself calmly in relation to past events. He can speak of them coherently, slowly, intelligibly and as he relates the story he remains calm while those who listen weep. Our art seeks to achieve this very result and requires that an actor experience the agony of his role . . . at home or in rehearsals, that he then calm himself . . . to convey to the audience in clear, pregnant, deeply felt, intelligible and eloquent terms what he has been through. At this point the spectators will be more affected than the actor.

—*An Actor Prepares*
—*Building a Character*

See ACTION, EXTERNAL TECHNIQUE, GIVEN CIRCUMSTANCES.

TRICKS—EFFECTIVE ADAPTATIONS

A contrivance or trick . . . is a vivid expression of inner feelings or thoughts. . . . It can call . . . attention to you, . . . prepare your partner by putting him in a mood to respond to you, . . . can transmit certain invisible messages, which can only be felt and not put into words, etc.

In using such means what we are primarily aiming at is to express our states of mind and heart in higher relief . . . [or] we make use of them to . . . mask our sensations. . . . If you follow an actor through a role . . . you may expect him, at a certain important point, to give his lines in a loud, clear-cut, serious tone of voice. Suppose that instead of that, he quite unexpectedly uses a light, gay and very soft tone. . . . The surprise element is . . . intriguing and effective. . . . Any number of actors . . . are capable of making brilliant adjustments and yet . . . use these means to entertain . . . rather than convey . . . feelings. They turn their powers of adaptation . . . into individual vaudeville numbers. . . . They are willing to sacrifice their role . . . to the excitement of obtaining a burst of applause, shouts of laughter. . . . Naturally . . . these adaptations lose all meaning.

—*An Actor Prepares*

See ADAPTATION.

TRUE ACTING

One cannot always create subconsciously and with inspiration. No such genius exists in the world. Therefore, our art teaches us first of all to create consciously and truly, because that will best prepare the way for the blossoming of the subconscious, which is inspiration. The more you have of conscious creative moments in your role the more chance you will have of a flow of inspiration. To play truly means to be right, logical, coherent, to think, strive, feel and act in unison with your role.

If you take all these internal processes, and adapt them to the spiritual and physical life of the person you are representing, we call that living the part.

To play truly, you must follow the course of right objectives, like posts to guide you across a treeless plain.

—An Actor Prepares

See ACTORS USE THEIR OWN FEELINGS, INSPIRATION, LOGIC AND CONTINUITY, PSYCHO-TECHNIQUE, SUBCONSCIOUS.

TUMBLING

Today we are adding tumbling to our activities. Although this may seem strange it helps an actor in his great moments of highest exaltation and creative inspiration. . . . The reason is that acrobatics aid in developing the quality of decisiveness. It would be too disastrous for an acrobat to go off wool gathering just before he performs a *salto mortale* or other neck-risking stunt. In such moments there is no room for indecision; he must, without stopping to reflect, give himself into the hands of chance and his skill. He must jump, come what may. This is exactly what an actor must do when he comes up to the culminating point of his role. . . . The actor cannot stop to think, to doubt, to weigh considerations, to make ready and test himself. He must act, he must clear the jump at full gallop.

Yet the majority of actors have an entirely different attitude about this. They dread the big moments, and long in advance they painstakingly try to prepare for them. This produces nervousness and pressures which prevent their letting themselves go at the high points, when they need to give themselves completely to their parts.

When you have developed will-power in your bodily movements and actions it will be easier for you to carry it over into living your role and you will learn how, without thinking, to surrender yourself instantly and utterly to the power of intuition and inspiration. . . . Besides, acrobatics can render you another service. They will help you to become more agile, more physically efficient on the stage when you get up, bend over, run and when you make a variety of difficult and rapid moves. They will teach you to act in a quick rhythm and tempo impossible for an untrained body.

—Building a Character

See BALLET, BODY TRAINING, EXTERNAL TECHNIQUE, PLASTICITY OF MOTION.

TYPE-CASTING

See CHARACTERISATION AND TRANSFORMATION, TYPES.

TYPES

In the world of dramatic art it has long been customary to divide actors into a number of categories: good, villainous, gay, suffering, bright, stupid, etc. This division of actors into groups is called type-casting. Therefore there are the following types: Tragedians (men and women), dramatic lovers, second-line lovers and dandies, dramatic and comic old men and women, noble fathers, character parts, moralists, comedians and simple-minded creatures, farce comedians, vaudeville lovers, *grandes dames*, dramatic and comic ingénues, vaudeville actors who can sing and play second- and third-rate parts.

The most ardent partisans of the custom of type-casting are the poorly endowed actors, whose range is not broad but rather one-sided. . . . Anyone who has even the most rudimentary external or inner gifts and experience on the stage can find one or two, even five roles, that he can play reasonably well if the main qualifications of these parts are suited to his own nature. All he has to do is to collect about ten such parts, differentiating them by changing his clothes, beards and wigs, and then he can qualify as an actor of such and such a type.

A true artist is of a different opinion: he does not hold with type-casting. . . . To my way of thinking there can be only one type of actor—the character actor. Perhaps this is beyond the powers of those who are not gifted. . . . Then they will be divided into only two categories: good actors and bad actors. . . . This is the best filter, one which will protect the theatre from being flooded with mediocrities.

People are always attracted by what they have not, and actors often use the stage to receive there what they cannot get in real life. . . . But the misunderstanding of one's true ability and calling in the art is the strongest obstacle in the further development of an actor. It is a blind alley which he enters for tens of years, and from which he cannot get out until he realizes his mistake and returns to the avenue that leads to the gates of pure art.

The roles for which you haven't the appropriate feelings are those you will never play well. . . . They will be excluded from your repertory. Actors are not in the main divided by types. The differences are made by their inner qualities.

—*An Actor Prepares*
—*Collected Works, Vol. V*
—*My Life in Art*
—*Stanislavski's Legacy*

See CHARACTERISATION AND TRANSFORMATION, EXTERNAL TECHNIQUE, LIMITATIONS.

U

UNBROKEN LINE

Our art . . . must have a whole, unbroken line . . . that flows from the past, through the present, into the future. . . . It is only when [an actor] comes to a deeper understanding of his part and a realization of its fundamental objective that a line gradually emerges as a continuous whole. Then we have the right to speak of the beginning of creative work.

On the stage, if the inner line is broken an actor no longer understands what is being said or done and he ceases to have any desires or emotions. The actor and the part, humanly speaking, live by these unbroken lines, that is what gives life and movement to what is being enacted. . . . A role must have continuous being and its unbroken line.

—*An Actor Prepares*

See SUPER-OBJECTIVE, THROUGH LINE OF ACTION.

UNITS, EPISODES

In order to work out the score of the play . . . we had to break it up into small units. . . . The technique of division is comparatively simple: What is the core [kernel] . . . the thing without which it cannot exist?

Remember the division is temporary. . . . It is only in preparation . . . that we use small units. During its [a play's] actual creation they fuse into large units. The larger and fewer the divisions, . . . the easier for you to handle the whole role.

As you put on your make-up you will think of the first unit. . . . You play the first one and are carried along to the next and the next.

Have you any conception of what a really good name for a unit is? It stands for its essential quality. To obtain it you must subject the unit to a process of crystallization. . . . The right name which crystallizes the essence of a unit, discovers its fundamental objective.

—An Actor Prepares

See OBJECTIVES, SCORE OF A ROLE.

UNTRUTH ON THE STAGE

A sense of truth contains within itself a sense of what is untrue as well. . . . It sets the pitch for you and shows you what you should not do. . . . Put a role on the right road and it will move ahead. It will grow broader and deeper and will in the end lead to inspiration . . . as . . . forced acting, clichés, and pretentiousness, untruth never can.

—An Actor Prepares
—Collected Works, Vol. II

See CLICHÉ ACTING, INSPIRATION, SENSE OF TRUTH ON THE STAGE.

V

VOICE

The work of voice placing consists primarily in the development of breathing and the vibration of sustained notes. It is often held that only vowels can be sustained. But do not consonants also possess this quality? Why should they not be developed to be as vibrant as vowels?

How good it would be if the teachers of singing simultaneously taught diction, and teachers of diction taught singing!

After many years of acting and directing experience I arrived at the full realization . . . that every actor must be in possession of excellent diction and pronunciation, that he must feel not only phrases and words but also each syllable, each letter.

To be "in good voice" is a blessing not only to a prima donna but also to the dramatic artist, . . . to have the feeling that you have the power to direct your sounds . . . know that they will forcibly convey the minutest details, modulations, shadings.

If the person who is to play Hamlet is obliged . . . to think about his deficiencies in voice . . . there is little likelihood of his being able to carry out his main creative undertaking.

"My voice is my fortune," said one famous actor . . . as he plunged his pocket thermometer into his soup . . . and other liquid refreshments. Out of concern for his voice, he felt impelled to watch the temperatures of everything he put in his mouth. This shows how much he cared about one of the greatest gifts of a creative nature—a beautiful, vibrant, expressive and powerful voice.

Salvini (said): "You need only three things [in order to become a tragedian]: Voice, voice, and more voice."

When you sense the possibilities opened up to you by a well-placed voice, capable of exercising its naturally predestined functions, the saying of Salvini will reveal to you its deep significance.

—Building a Character
—My Life in Art

See SPEECH, VOICE VOLUME.

VOICE VOLUME

Volume is not to be sought in high tension use of the voice, not in loudness or shouting, but in raising and lowering . . . intonations, . . . in the gradual expansion from piano to forte and in their mutual relationship.

—Building a Character

See ACCENTUATION, INTONATIONS AND PUNCTUATION, PAUSES IN SPEECH, SPEECH, VOICE.

W

WALKING ON THE STAGE

On the stage, we are obliged to walk correctly as nature intended. . . . People whom nature has not endowed with a good normal gait . . . resort to all kinds of strategems to conceal this shortcoming. They . . . walk in some special way, with unnatural form and picturesqueness. Yet that kind of theatrical, stagey walk is not to be confused with a true stage walk based on natural laws. . . . Let us learn to walk all over again from the beginning, both on the stage and off.

—*Building a Character*

See PLASTICITY OF MOTION.

WHAT IS MY SYSTEM?

My system is the result of lifelong searchings. . . . I have groped after a method of work for actors which will enable them to create the image of a character, breathe into it the life of a human spirit and, by natural means, embody it on the stage in a beautiful, artistic form. . . . The foundations for this method were my studies of the nature of an actor.

The *first* [proposition] is this: There are no formulas . . . on how to become a great actor, or how to play this or that part. [It] is made up of steps towards the true creative state of an actor on the stage. When it is true it is the . . . normal state of a person in real life. But to achieve that normal living state . . . an actor

. . . has to be: (a) physically free, in control of free muscles; (b) his attention must be infinitely alert; (c) he must be able to listen and observe on the stage as he would in real life, that is to say be in contact with the person playing opposite him; (d) he must believe in everything that is happening on the stage that is related to the play.

The *second proposition* . . . is: A true inner creative state on the stage makes it possible for an actor to execute actions necessary for him to take in accordance with the terms of the play, whether inner psychological actions or external, physical ones. . . . Actually in each physical act there is an inner psychological motive which impels physical action, as in every psychological inner action there is also physical action, which expresses its psychic nature.

The union of these two actions results in organic action on the stage.

That action then is determined by the subject of the play, its idea, the character of a certain part and the circumstances set up by the playwright.

In order to make it easier for you as an actor to take action on the stage, put yourself first of all in the circumstances proposed by the playwright for the character you are playing. Ask yourself: what would I do *if* the same thing should happen to me as it does in the play to the character I am playing? . . . Find out all the reasons which justify the actions of your character and then act without reflecting about just where your "own" actions end and "his" begin.

The *third* proposition (is): True organic action . . . is bound to give rise to sincere feelings.

Therefore the summing up is: *On the stage a true inner creative state, action and feeling result in natural life on the stage in the form of one of the characters.*

It is by this means that you will come closest to what we call "metamorphosis," always providing of course that you have properly understood the play, its idea, its subject and plot, and have shaped inside yourself the character of one of the dramatis personae.

The power of this method lies in the fact that it was not . . . invented, . . . it is based on the laws of nature.

The system is not a hand-me-down suit you can put on and walk off in. . . . It is a whole way of life; you have to educate yourself in it. . . . You cannot hope to do this all at once.

With strong desire, if you work, if you come to know your own nature, and discipline it, then with talent you will become a true artist.

With the gradual study of the method . . . you will find it is not as complicated in execution as it may appear to be in theory. My system is for all nations. All peoples possess the same human nature: it manifests itself in varying ways, but my system is no deterrent to that.

—*An Actor Prepares*
—*Building a Character*
—*Stanislavski's Legacy*